Requirements Engineering Fundamentals
2nd Edition

About the Authors

Klaus Pohl holds a full professorship for Software Systems Engineering at the Institute for Computer Science and Business Information Systems (ICB) at University of Duisburg-Essen, Germany. He was the scientific funding director of Lero, the Irish Software Engineering Research Centre. Currently he is the acting director of paluno—The Ruhr Institute for Software Technology—at the University of Duisburg-Essen. He received his Ph.D. and his habilitation in computer science from RWTH Aachen, Germany.

Klaus is (co-)author of more than 250 peer-reviewed publications and several text books. He served as Program and General Chair for many international and national conferences including the 35th ACM/IEEE Conference on Software Engineering (ICSE 2013). As consultant, assessor, and expert he supports small and multi-national companies, research institutes, and public funded research programs. Klaus is co-founder of the IREB e.V. (International Requirements Engineering Board). You can find more information on https://sse.uni-due.de.

Chris Rupp—SOPHIST-in-chief (formally: founder and executive partner of the SOPHIST GmbH), chief consultant, coach and trainer. Looking back over 25 years of professional experience, a lot has come up: a company… 6 books… 55 employees… countless articles and presentations… and a whole lot of experience. My passion for project consultation might account for the fact that, until now, I do not "only" manage, but I am still directly involved in projects and close to customers. What drives me is the vision to implement good ideas so that developers, contractual partners and users—both direct and indirect—face an intelligent, sophisticated and beneficial product. In doing so, I work with a range of methods and approaches in agile and non-agile environments.

In order to standardize qualification for requirements engineers / business analysts, I founded the IREB e.V. (International Requirements Engineering Board). You can find further information on www.sophist.de.

Klaus Pohl · Chris Rupp

Requirements Engineering Fundamentals

A Study Guide for the Certified Professional
for Requirements Engineering Exam

Foundation Level – IREB compliant

2nd Edition

Klaus Pohl (klaus.pohl@sse.uni-due.de)
Chris Rupp (chris.rupp@sophist.de)

Translated from German by Thorsten Weyer, Bastian Tenbergen, and Marta Tayeh.
Editor: Michael Barabas
Project Manager: Matthias Rossmanith
Copyeditor: Judy Flynn
Proofreader: James Johnson
Layout and Type: Josef Hegele
Cover design: Helmut Kraus, www.exclam.de

ISBN 978-1-937538-77-4

2nd Edition (2nd Printing, December 2016)
© 2015 by Klaus Pohl and Chris Rupp

Rocky Nook Inc.
1010 B Street, Ste. 350
San Rafael, CA 94901

www.rockynook.com

Library of Congress Cataloging-in-Publication Data

Pohl, Klaus.
 Requirements engineering fundamentals : a study guide for the certified professional for requirements
engineering exam, foundation level, IREB compliant / Klaus Pohl, Chris Rupp. -- 2nd edition.
    pages cm
 ISBN 978-1-937538-77-4 (softcover : alk. paper)
1. Software engineering--Examinations--Study guides. 2. System design--Examinations--Study guides.
3. Requirements engineering--Examinations--Study guides. 4. Electronic data processing documentation--
Examinations--Study guides. I. Rupp, Chris. II. Title.
 QA76.758.P6413 2015
 005.1076--dc23
                        2015009245

Foreword

Dear reader,

With *Requirements Engineering Fundamentals*, you are holding the official text book of the *Certified Professional for Requirements Engineering (CPRE) – Foundation Level* certification in your hands.

The 2nd edition of this book is aligned with the curriculum (version 2.2) of the International Requirements Engineering Board e.V. (IREB) and the IREB glossary. In addition, some minor defects of the 1st edition have been corrected. A short introduction to the IREB and the certification process can be found in the previous section "The Certified Professional for Requirements Engineering (CPRE) Exam".

The aim of this book is to aid you in your preparation for the certification examination of the Certified Professional for Requirements Engineering. The book is suited for your individual preparation for the examination as well as for companion literature to training courses offered by training providers.

In addition to the book, you should consider the information about the preparation for the certification examination published on the IREB website (http://www.ireb.org/en). That additional information reflects updates of the curriculum (after version 2.2) and potentially amends this book with respect to some areas of interest. Errata to this book are published on the IREB website.

Our decision to author this book collaboratively was not unjustified. The book at hand is meant to integrate long-lasting practical experiences with educational and research knowledge concerning the topic of requirements engineering, in particular for the Foundation Level of the Certified Professional for Requirements Engineering. As a consequence, this book is based on the two best-selling books in the German language about requirements engineering by the two main authors:

Klaus Pohl: *Requirements Engineering – Grundlagen, Prinzipien, Techniken.* Published at dpunkt.verlag, Heidelberg, 2008. This book was written from a perspective of research and education and offers a structured discussion of the fundamentals, principles, and techniques of requirements engineering. (Also available in English: *Requirements Engineering – Fundamentals, Principles, and Techniques.* Springer, New York, 2010)

Chris Rupp: *Requirements-Engineering und -Management – Aus der Praxis von klassisch bis agil.* Published at Hanser Fachbuchverlag, Munich, 2014. This book contains application-oriented knowledge about requirements engineering, which supports the requirements engineer in his or her daily practice. (Individual chapters also available in English on the SOPHIST website: http://www.sophist.de)

We have chosen not to reference the two books listed above in the individual chapters of this book. You can find detailed additional information on the topics of this book in both of the books mentioned above.

This book was made possible with the help of a number of people. Our special thanks go to Dirk Schüpferling and Thorsten Weyer for their contributions to this book and their outstanding commitment, without which this book would not have been possible. Many reviews and consistent support by other board members increased the quality of this book. We particularly thank all board members of the IREB for their active support. In addition, Urte Pautz of the Siemens AG; Christian Pikalek and Rainer Joppich of the SOPHIST GmbH (www.sophist.de); and Dr. Kim Lauenroth and Nelufar Ulfat-Bunyadi from "paluno – The Ruhr Institute for Software Technology" at the University of Duisburg-Essen (www.paluno.de) have contributed to individual sections of the book. Furthermore, we want to thank Thorsten Weyer and Bastian Tenbergen (paluno) as well as Marta Tayeh (SOPHIST GmbH) for their commitment towards translating this book from German into English. Thanks also to Philipp Schmidt and Dirk Schüpferling for their support in aligning this book to the IREB syllabus version 2.2.

We also want to thank Christa Preisendanz, Dr. Michael Barabas, and Judy Flynn for their support in publishing this book.

Klaus Pohl and Chris Rupp
Essen and Nuremberg, February 2015

With Contributions from

Karol Frühauf
INFOGEM AG, SAQ

Karol Frühauf studied in Bratislava and at RWTH Aachen, gaining his degree in computer engineering in 1975. He then spent 12 years at Brown, Boveri & Cie working as a programmer, head of quality and finally as a manager in network control technology. In 1987, Frühauf founded INFOGEM AG with Helmut Sandmayr, and the company has since gained a reputation as one of the leading system engineering consulting and training addresses in Switzerland. He is an honorary member of SAQ, the Swiss Association for Quality and was instrumental in the launch of the "Brückenwächter" ("Bridge Guard") residence for artists and scientists in Štúrovo, Slovakia.

Emmerich Fuchs
FUCHS-INFORMATIK AG

Emmerich Fuchs has over 30 years of experience in application development. Since 1985, he has been working as a lecturer at schools of higher education and as a seminar instructor as well as a co-author of many books and an examination expert. In 1989, he founded the FUCHS-INFORMATIK AG and is now working as a consulting business manager for renowned companies in the areas of business process modeling, requirements engineering, and quality assurance.

Prof. Dr. Martin Glinz
University of Zurich

Martin Glinz is a full professor of computer science and leads the research unit Requirements Engineering at the University of Zurich. He is mainly interested in methods, languages and tools for requirement modeling. His additional fields of interest include software engineering, software quality, and modeling. He obtained his doctoral degree from RWTH Aachen in computer science. Before he accepted the call to Zurich, he worked for over 10 years in the industry as a researcher, developer, consultant, and lecturer in the field of software engineering. He is a member of the board of publishers of *Requirements Engineering* and a member of the International Requirements Engineering Board (IREB). He was chairman of the steering committee for the International Requirements Engineering Conference from 2007–2009.

Rainer Grau
Digitec Galaxus

Rainer Grau is Head of Business Development at Digitec/Galaxus, one of Switzerland's top eCommerce companies. He and his team are responsible for innovation and portfolio management as well as the implementation of all the company's strategic projects. Before joining Digitec/Galaxus he was a director and partner at Zühlke Engineering, where he was in charge of agility, lean management, requirements engineering and product management.

Rainer Grau holds various teaching posts at Swiss universities and is actively involved in SAQ, the Swiss Association for Quality. He is a founder member of the Swiss Agile Leaders Circle where he supports community members in their requirements engineering, enterprise agility and lean management activities.

Rainer Grau likes to spend his free time with his family, on his bicycle, windsurfing, rock climbing or reading the latest novels by T.C. Boyle and Haruki Murakami.

Colin Hood
*Colin Hood Systems
Engineering Ltd.*

Starting out in 1977, Colin Hood has accompanied the evolution of control systems from their beginnings in relay-based systems through programmable logic controllers (PLCs) to modern software-controlled safety-critical systems. His various jobs have included analysis, design, implementation, testing and delivery of complex software systems. Requirements engineering has always been the foundation of his success at companies such as Alcatel, BMW, DaimlerChrysler, Hella and Miele. As well as continually improving the processes involved, he specializes in introducing new methods and tools that support the process of change.

Dr. Frank Houdek
Daimler AG

Frank Houdek graduated in Computer Science at the University of Ulm and joined the Daimler Research Centre in 1995. After completing his PhD in empirical software engineering in 1999 he began working in requirements engineering and has headed various research and technology transfer projects within the Daimler passenger car and commercial vehicles business units. Since 2013 he has been responsible for coordinating the requirements engineering activities for all electric/electronic specifications in Mercedes-Benz passenger car development.

Dr. Houdek is a member of GI (German Interest Group on Computer Science) and IEEE CS, and belongs to the steering committee of the GI Group 2.1.6 (Requirements Engineering). He is also involved in the organizational and program committees for requirements engineering events such as RE, REFSQ, and ICSE.

He is responsible for the *Requirements Engineering* module of the *Software Engineering for Embedded Systems* course at the Technical University at Kaiserslautern.

Dr. Peter Hruschka
Atlantic Systems Guild

Peter Hruschka has been working as an independent IT and management consultant since 1994. His mission is the practical implementation of new ideas in software engineering. This comprises the entire spectrum from analysis of the initial situation via the creation of strategic plans to introductory training for every (structured or object-oriented) method and process to guarantee success. Dr. Hruschka is principal of the Atlantic Systems Guild, an internationally renowned group of experts on software technology, and founder of the German network of agile developers.

Prof. Dr. Barbara Paech
University of Heidelberg

Barbara Paech is a professor with the Institute for Computer Science of the University of Heidelberg. Until October 2003, she was a department leader with the Fraunhofer Institute for Experimental Software Engineering. Her area of research is software engineering, especially the methods and processes necessary to improve quality with appropriate effort. For many years, she has been active in the area of requirements engineering and usability engineering. Paech and her group have implemented many national, international and industrial research and technology transfer projects. She is a member of the International Requirements Engineering Board (IREB).

Dirk Schüpferling
SOPHIST GmbH

I am a SOPHIST since 2001 and the past years have led me to the conclusion that, in most cases, communication is the key to (customer) satisfaction. What surprised me was that features like laziness or being a know-it-all can—applied correctly— lead to something positive. The specialist calls this "reuse" or "identifying potential for improvement". I transmit this knowledge as a classic Requirements-Engineer, as well as in agile contexts (e.g., as Product Owner) in various projects. My job is to support the project team in the conception or application of new methods.

Thorsten Weyer
University of Duisburg-Essen

Thorsten Weyer is a research group leader at the University of Duisburg-Essen and Head of Requirements Engineering and Conceptual Design at "paluno – The Ruhr Institute for Software Technology" at the University of Duisburg-Essen. He has worked for more than a decade as a researcher and consultant in requirements engineering, systems analysis, variability management, and model-based software engineering. He is a member of the organizational and program committees for various scientific conferences and also contributes his expertise to research funding projects and international trade publications. Thorsten Weyer is a member of the International Requirements Engineering Board (IREB) and co-publisher of the *Requirements Engineering Magazine*.

Contents

1 Introduction and Foundations

The impact of requirements engineering (RE) on successful and customer-oriented systems development can no longer be ignored. It has become common practice to provide resources for requirements engineering. In addition, there is a growing understanding that the role of the requirements engineer is essentially self-contained and comprises a series of demanding activities.

1.1 Introduction

According to the figures reported in the Standish Group's Chaos Report of 2006, much has improved in the execution of software projects in the twelve years between 1994 and 2006. While about 30 percent of the software projects investigated in 1994 failed, it was a mere 20 percent in 2006. The number of projects that exceeded time or budget constraints significantly and/or did not meet customer satisfaction dropped from 53 percent to 46 percent [Chaos 2006]. Jim Johnson, chairperson of the Standish Group, names three reasons for the positive development of the figures since 1994. One is that the communication of requirements has much improved since ten years ago. These figures are of importance since how the requirements of a system are handled is a significant cause for project failures and/or time and budget overruns.

Why perform requirements engineering?

1.1.1 Figures and Facts from Ordinary Projects

According to past studies, approximately 60 percent of all errors in system development projects originate during the phase of requirements engineering [Boehm 1981]. These errors, however, are often discovered only in later project phases or once the system has been deployed because incorrect or incomplete requirements can be interpreted by developers in such a fashion that they are subjectively sound or (subconsciously) complete. Missing requirements often remain undetected during design and

Requirements engineering as a cause of errors

realization because developers trust the requirements engineers to deliver high-quality work. Developers implement whatever the requirements document says or what they believe it to be saying. Unclear, incomplete, or wrong requirements inevitably lead to the development of a system that does not possess critical properties or possesses properties that were not requested.

Costs of errors during requirements engineering

The later in the development project a defect in the requirements is corrected, the higher are the costs associated with fixing it. For instance, the effort to fix a requirements defect is up to 20 times higher if the correction is done during programming as opposed to fixing the same defect during requirements engineering. If the defect is fixed during acceptance testing, the effort involved may be up to a 100 times higher [Boehm 1981].

Symptoms and causes of deficient requirements engineering

Symptoms for inadequate requirements engineering are as numerous as their causes. Frequently, requirements are missing or not clearly formulated. For instance, if the requirements do not reflect customer wishes precisely or if the requirements are described in an imprecise way and thus allow for several interpretations, the result is often a system that does not meet the expectations of the client or the users.

The most common reason for deficient requirements is the misconception of the stakeholders that much is self-evident and does not need to be stated explicitly. This results in problems in communication among the involved parties that arise from differences in experience and knowledge. To make matters worse, it is often the case that especially the client wishes for quick integration of recent results into a productive system.

The significance of good requirements engineering

The increasing importance of software-intensive systems in industrial projects as well as the need to bring more innovative, more individual, and more comprehensive systems to market and the need to do so quicker, better, and with a higher level of quality calls for efficient requirements engineering. Complete requirements free from defects are the basis for successful system development. Potential risks have to be identified during requirements engineering and must be reduced as early as possible to allow for successful project progress. Faults and gaps in requirement documents must be discovered early on to avoid tedious change processes.

1.1.2   Requirements Engineering – What Is It?

In order to make a development project succeed, it is necessary to know the requirements for the system and to document them in a suitable manner.

Definition 1-1: *Requirement*

(1) A condition or capability needed by a user to solve a problem or achieve an objective.

(2) A condition or capability that must be met or possessed by a system or system component to satisfy a contract, standard, specification, or other formally imposed documents.

(3) A documented representation of a condition or capability as in (1) or (2).

[IEEE 610.12-1990]

The term *stakeholder* is essential in requirements engineering. Among other things, stakeholders are the most important sources of requirements. Not considering a stakeholder often results in fragmentally elicited requirements, i.e., incomplete requirements [Macaulay 1993]. Stakeholders are those people or organizations that have some impact on the requirements. This could be people that are going to interact with the system (e.g., users or administrators), people that have a mere interest in the system but are not likely to use it (e.g., the management, a hacker from which the system must be protected, stakeholders of competing systems), but also legal entities, institutions, etc., because these are embodied by living people who may choose to influence or define the requirements of the system.

Stakeholders

Definition 1-2: *Stakeholder*

A stakeholder of a system is a person or an organization that has an (direct or indirect) influence on the requirements of the system.

During the development process, requirements engineering must elicit the stakeholders' requirements, document the requirements in a suitable manner, validate and verify the requirements, and manage the requirements over the course of the entire life cycle of the system [Pohl 1996].

Goal of requirements engineering

> **Definition 1-3:** *Requirements Engineering*
>
> (1) Requirements engineering is a systematic and disciplined approach to the specification and management of requirements with the following goals:
>
> > (1.1) Knowing the relevant requirements, achieving a consensus among the stakeholders about these requirements, documenting them according to given standards, and managing them systematically
> >
> > (1.2) Understanding and documenting the stakeholders' desires and needs, they specifying and managing requirements to minimize the risk of delivering a system that does not meet the stakeholders' desires and needs

Four core activities of requirements engineering

The four core activities to meet these ends are as follows:

- *Elicitation:* During requirements elicitation, different techniques are used to obtain requirements from stakeholders and other sources and to refine the requirements in greater detail.
- *Documentation:* During documentation, the elicited requirements are described adequately. Different techniques are used to document the requirements by using natural language or conceptual models (see chapters 4, 5, and 6).
- *Validation and negotiation:* In order to guarantee that the predefined quality criteria are met, documented requirements must be validated and negotiated early on (see chapter 7).
- *Management:* Requirements management is orthogonal to all other activities and comprises any measures that are necessary to structure requirements, to prepare them so that they can be used by different roles, to maintain consistency after changes, and to ensure their implementation (see chapter 8).

These core activities can be applied for different levels of requirements abstraction, like stakeholder requirements, system requirements, and software requirements. Their execution can follow different processes, such as the processes recommended in [ISO/IEC/IEEE 29148:2011].

Constraints   Different project constraints influence requirements engineering. For instance, people, domain factors, or organizational constraints (e.g., spatial distribution or temporal availability of project members) have a large impact on the choice of suitable techniques.

1.1.3   Embedding Requirements Engineering into Process Models

Ponderous process models (e.g., the Waterfall model [Royce 1987] or the V-Model [V-Modell 2004]) aim at completely eliciting and documenting all requirements in an early project phase before any design or realization decisions are made. The goal of such models is to elicit all requirements prior to the actual development. As a result, in these process models, requirements engineering is understood to be a finite, time-restricted initial phase of system development.

Requirements engineering as a self-contained phase

Lightweight process models (e.g., eXtreme Programming [Beck 1999]), on the other hand, only elicit necessary requirements once they are supposed to be implemented as "foretelling" future functionalities is difficult and requirements change over the course of the project. In these process models, requirements engineering is treated as a continuous, comprehensive process that comprises and integrates all phases of system development.

Requirements engineering as a continuous, collateral process

1.2   Fundamentals of Communication Theory

Requirements must be communicated. In most cases, one uses a rule-driven medium that is accessible to the communication partner—natural language.

Language as a medium for requirement communication

For the transmission of information from one individual to another to work properly, a common code is needed. The sender encodes her message and the receiver has to decode it. Such a common code is intrinsic to any two people that speak the same language (e.g., German), have the same cultural background, and have similar experiences. The more similar the cultural and educational background, the area of expertise, and the everyday work life, the better the exchange of information works. However, such ideal conditions most often do not exist between stakeholders. It is therefore sensible to agree upon a common language and how this common language is to be used. This can, for instance, be achieved by means of glossaries (see chapter 4), in which all important terms are explained. Alternatively, this can be done by agreeing upon a formal descriptive language, e.g., OMG's Unified Modeling Language, UML (see chapter 6).

Another important factor is the type of communication medium. In verbal communication, the success of the communication relies heavily on redundancy (e.g., language and gestures or language and intonation) and

Type of communication medium

feedback. In written technical communication, for example, information is transmitted with a minimum of redundancy and feedback.

Language comfort   In addition to the problems arising from differing domain vocabularies and different communication media, it can often be observed that information is not adequately transmitted or not transmitted at all. This can be traced back to natural transformations that occur during human perception. These transformational effects are, in particular, *focusing* and *simplification* and can impact the communication more or less harshly.

Implicit background knowledge   Communication—i.e., the language-based expression of knowledge—is necessarily simplifying in nature. The author expects the reader to have some kind of implicit background knowledge. It is the simplifications that arise from language-based knowledge expression that become problematic with regard to requirements, as requirements can become interpretable in different ways. In chapter 5, natural language-based requirement documentation is discussed in further detail.

1.3   Characteristics of a Requirements Engineer

Central role   The requirements engineer as a project role is often at the center of attention. She is usually the only one who has direct contact with the stakeholders and has both the ability and the responsibility to become as familiar as possible with the domain and to understand it as well as possible. She is the one that identifies the needs underlying the stakeholders' statements and amends them in a way that architects and developers—usually laymen where the domain in question is concerned—can understand and implement them. The requirements engineer is, in a manner of speaking, a translator that understands the domain as well as its particular language well enough and also possesses enough IT know-how to be aware of the problems the developers face and to be able to communicate with them on the same level. The requirements engineer therefore has a central role in the project.

Seven necessary capabilities of a requirements engineer   To be able to fulfill all of her tasks, the requirements engineer needs much more than process knowledge. Many of the capabilities required must be based on practical experience.

- *Analytic thinking*: The requirements engineer must be able to become familiar with domains that are unknown to her and must understand and analyze complicated problems and relationships. Since stakeholders often discuss problematic requirements by means of concrete examples and (suboptimal) solutions, the requirements engineer must be able to abstract from the concrete statements of the stakeholder.

- *Empathy:* The requirements engineer has the challenging task of identifying the actual needs of a stakeholder. A core requirement to be able to achieve this is to have good intuition and empathy for people. In addition, she must identify problems that might arise in a group of stakeholders and act accordingly.
- *Communication skills:* To elicit the requirements from stakeholders and to interpret them correctly and communicate them in a suitable manner, a requirements engineer must have good communication skills. She must be able to listen, ask the right questions at the right time, notice when a statement does not contain the desired information, and make further inquiries when necessary.
- *Conflict resolution skills:* Different opinions of different stakeholders can be the cause of conflicts during requirements engineering. The requirements engineer must identify conflicts, mediate between the parties involved, and apply techniques suitable to resolving the conflict.
- *Moderation skills:* The requirements engineer must be able to mediate between different opinions and lead discussions. This holds true for individual conversations as well as group conversations and workshops.
- *Self-confidence:* Since the requirements engineer is frequently at the center of attention, she occasionally is exposed to criticism as well. As a result, she needs a high level of self-confidence and the ability to defend herself should strong objections to her opinions arise. She should never take criticism personally.
- *Persuasiveness:* Among other things, the requirements engineer is, in a matter of speaking, a kind of attorney for the requirements of the stakeholders. She must be able to represent the requirements in team meetings and presentations. In addition, she must consolidate differing opinions, facilitate a decision in case of a disagreement, and create consensus among the stakeholders.

1.4   Requirement Types

Generally, one can distinguish between three types of requirements:

- *Functional requirements* define the functionality that the system to be developed offers. Usually, these requirements are divided into functional requirements, behavioral requirements, and data requirements (see chapter 4).

> **Definition 1-4:** *Functional Requirement*
>
> A functional requirement is a requirement concerning a result of behavior that shall be provided by a function of the system.

- *Quality requirements* define desired qualities of the system to be developed and often influence the system architecture more than functional requirements do. Typically, quality requirements are about the performance, availability, dependability, scalability, or portability of a system. Requirements of this type are frequently classified as non-functional requirements.

> **Definition 1-5:** *Quality Requirement*
>
> A quality requirement is a requirement that pertains to a quality concern that is not covered by functional requirements.

- *Constraints* cannot be influenced by the team members. Requirements of this type can constrain the system itself (e.g., "The system shall be implemented using web services") or the development process ("The system shall be available on the market no later than the second quarter of 2012"). In contrast to functional and quality requirements, constraints are not implemented, they are adhered to because they merely limit the solution space available during the development process.

> **Definition 1-6:** *Constraint*
>
> A constraint is a requirement that limits the solution space beyond what is necessary for meeting the given functional requirements and quality requirements.

In addition to the classification into functional requirements, quality requirements, and constraints, a number of different classifications of requirements are used in practice. For example, there are a number of classifications suggested by several standards, e.g., CMMI [SEI 2006] or SPICE [ISO/IEC 15504-5]. Other classification schemes describe requirement attributes, such as the level of detail of a requirement, the priority, or the degree of legal obligation of requirements (see chapters 4 and 8).

1.5   Importance and Categorization of Quality Requirements

In daily practice, quality requirements of a system are often not documented, inadequately documented, or improperly negotiated. Such circumstances can threaten the project's success or the subsequent acceptance of the system under development. Therefore, the requirements engineer should place special emphasis on the elicitation, documentation, and negotiation of quality requirements during the development process.

Typically, many different kinds of desired qualities of the system are assigned to the requirement type *quality requirement*. In order to be able to deal with quality requirements in a structured manner, many different classification schemes for quality requirements have been proposed. The ISO/IEC 25010:2011 standard [ISO/IEC 25010:2011], for example, suggests a classification scheme for quality requirements that can also be used as a standard structure for requirements documentation and as a checklist for requirements elicitation and validation. Among others, the following categories are typical for quality requirements (see [ISO/IEC 25010:2011]):

- Requirements that define the performance of the system, in particular response time behavior and resource utilization
- Requirements that define the security of the system, in particular with regard to accountability, authenticity, confidentiality, and integrity
- Requirements that define the reliability of functionalities, in particular with regard to availability, fault tolerance, and recoverability
- Requirements that define the usability of a system, in particular with regard to accessibility, learnability, and ease of use
- Requirements that define the maintainability of a system, in particular with regard to reusability, analyzability, changeability, and testability

- Requirements that define the portability of a system, in particular with regard to adaptability, installability, and replaceability

Currently, quality requirements are often specified using natural language. However, numerous approaches to document quality requirements by means of models have been suggested over the past couple of years.

The requirements engineer is responsible for making sure the quality requirements are as objective and verifiable as possible. Typically, this necessitates that the quality requirements are quantified. For example, a quality requirement with regard to system performance could specify that a system shall process 95 percent of all queries within 1.5 seconds and that it must not take longer than 4 seconds to process queries at any given time. This can cause quality requirements to be refined by means of additional functional requirements. This could be the case for a quality requirement that is concerned with system security if a functional requirement specifies the exact encryption algorithm to satisfy the need for encryption as demanded by some quality requirement.

Quality requirements are often related to different functional requirements. As a result, quality requirements should always be kept separated from functional requirements. In other words, quality requirements should not be mixed with functional requirements and should be documented separately, with explicit documentation of their relation to functional requirements.

1.6 Summary

Requirements engineering can hardly be avoided, especially when systems are to be developed that satisfy customers and meet budget constraints and schedules. The goal of requirements engineering is to document customer requirements as completely as possible in good quality and to identify and resolve problems in the requirements as early as possible. Successful requirements engineering is based on including the right stakeholders as well as embedding the four core activities of requirements engineering (*elicitation, documentation, validation and negotiation,* and *management*) into the system development process. At the center of attention is the requirements engineer, who is the primary contact point in requirements engineering and possesses a great deal of domain knowledge and process knowledge as well as a multitude of soft skills.

2 System and Context Boundaries

The requirements for a system to be developed do not simply exist, they have to be elicited. The purpose of defining the system and context boundaries in requirements engineering is to identify the part of the environment that influences the requirements for the system to be developed.

2.1 System Context

In the development process, requirements engineering fulfils the task of identifying all those material and immaterial aspects that have a relationship to the system. In order to do that, it is anticipated what the system will be like once it becomes real. By doing so, those parts of the real world which will potentially influence the requirements of the system can be identified. To be able to specify the requirements for a system correctly and completely, it is necessary to identify the relationships between individual material and immaterial aspects as precisely as possible. The part of reality that is relevant for the requirements of a system is called the system context.

Anticipate the system in operation

> **Definition 2-1:** *System Context*
>
> The system context is the part of the system environment that is relevant for the definition as well as the understanding of the requirements of a system to be developed.

Among others, the following possible aspects of reality influence the context of a system:

Context aspects in the system context

- People (stakeholders or groups of stakeholders)
- Systems in operation (other technical systems or hardware)
- Processes (technical or physical processes, business processes)
- Events (technical or physical)
- Documents (e.g., laws, standards, system documentation)

Consequence of erroneous or incomplete context consideration

If the system context is incorrectly or incompletely considered during requirements engineering, it may result in incomplete or erroneous requirements. This leads to the system operating on the basis of incomplete or erroneous requirements, which is often the reason for system failure during operation. Such errors often remain undetected during the validation procedures, which determine if the system meets the specified requirements, and occur only during operation, sometimes entailing catastrophic consequences.

System context and requirement context

The origin of the system's requirements lies within the context of the system to be developed. For example, stakeholders, pertinent standards, and legal guidelines demand particular functional properties that the system to be developed must possess at its interfaces. A requirement is therefore defined for a specific context and can only be interpreted correctly in regard to this specific context. The better the context of a requirement is understood (e.g., why is the technical system "X" in the system context the origin of some requirement), the lower the likelihood of incorrect interpretation of the requirement. Therefore, a purpose-driven documentation of the system context or information about the system context is of particular importance.

2.2   Defining System and Context Boundaries

It is within the responsibility of the requirements engineer to define the system context properly. In order to do so, it is necessary to separate the system context from the system to be developed as well as from the parts of reality that are irrelevant for the system (see figure 2-1):

- *Defining the system boundary:* When defining the system boundary, a decision has to be made: Which aspects pertain to the system to be developed and which aspects belong in the system context?
- *Defining the context boundary:* When defining the context boundary, the question to be answered is: Which aspects pertain to the system context (i.e., have a relation to the system to be developed) and which aspects are part of the irrelevant environment?

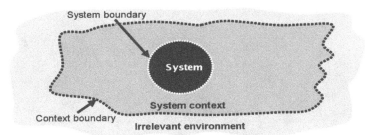

Figure 2-1 *System and context boundary of a system*

Thus, system and context boundaries define the system context. The system context comprises all aspects that are relevant with regard to the requirements for the system to be developed. These aspects cannot be altered or modified by the system development process.

System and context boundaries define the system context.

2.2.1   Defining the System Boundary

The system boundary separates the object of concern (i.e., the system) from its environment. When the system boundary is defined, the scope of the development (i.e., the aspects that are covered by the system to be developed) as well as the aspects that are not part of the system are determined. We therefore define the system boundary as follows:

Definition 2-2: *System Boundary*

The system boundary separates the system to be developed from its environment; i.e., it separates the part of the reality that can be modified or altered by the development process from aspects of the environment that cannot be changed or modified by the development process.

All aspects that are within the system boundary can thus be altered during system development. For instance, an existing system that consists of hardware and software components and is supposed to be replaced by the new system can be within the system boundary. Aspects within the system context can be business processes, technical processes, people and roles, organizational structures, and components of the IT infrastructure. Figure 2-2 schematically shows the system context of a system. The system context consists of other systems, groups of stakeholders that in some way use the interfaces of the system to be developed, and additional requirements sources and their interrelations.

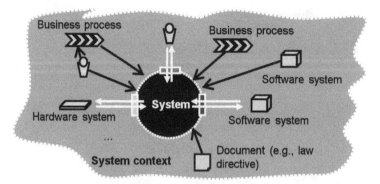

Figure 2-2 *Types of aspects within the system context*

Sources and sinks as the
starting point

Among other things, sources and sinks (see, e.g., [DeMarco 1978]) can be used to identify the interfaces the system has with its environment. Sources provide inputs for the system. Sinks receive outputs from the system. Possible sources and sinks of a system are as follows:

- (Groups of) stakeholders
- Existing systems (both technical and nontechnical systems)

Interfaces: interaction between
system and environment

Sources and sinks interact with the system to be developed via system interfaces. Using these interfaces, the system provides its functionality to the environment, monitors the environment, influences parameters of the environment, and controls operations of the environment. Depending on the type of the respective source or sink, the system needs different interface types (e.g., human–machine interface, hardware interface, or software interface). The interface type in turn may also impose specific constraints or additional sources of requirements on the system to be developed.

Gray zone between system
and system context

Frequently, the system boundary is not precisely defined until the end of the requirements engineering process. Before that, some or several interfaces as well as desired functions and qualities of the system to be developed are only partially known or not known at all. We refer to this initially vague separation of the system and its context as the gray zone between the system and the context (see figure 2-3). At the beginning of the requirements engineering process, it may, for example, not be clear whether the system should implement a certain function (e.g., "pay by credit card") or whether there is another system in the system context providing such a function that should be used (e.g., "payment processing").

The system boundary may not only shift within the gray zone (① in figure 2-3) but also the gray zone itself may shift during the requirements engineering process (② in figure 2-3). This kind of shifting is caused by the fact that aspects, pertaining at first to the system context, now will be modified during system development. Such a situation occurs during requirements engineering, for example, if it is not clear in the system context whether certain activities of a business process should be implemented or supported by the system to be developed or not. In this situation, it is not clear which aspects belong to the system and can thus be changed or modified and which aspects belong to the system context. This causes a corresponding shift of the gray zone between system and system context (see figure 2-3).

Adjusting the gray zone

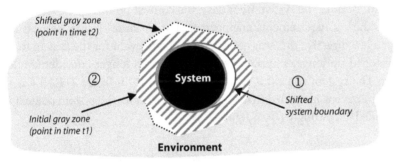

Figure 2-3 *Gray zone of the system boundary*

The gray zone shifts, for instance, when interfaces are attributed to the system boundary and the gray zone is extended to comprise aspects of the environment that concern these interfaces.

2.2.2 Defining the Context Boundary

The context boundary distinguishes between context aspects, i.e., those aspects of the environment that need to be taken into account during requirements engineering (e.g., as requirements sources) and those aspects that are irrelevant for the system. The context boundary can be defined as follows:

> **Definition 2-3:** *Context Boundary*
>
> The context boundary separates the relevant part of the environment of a system to be developed from the irrelevant part, i.e., the part that does not influence the system to be developed and, thus, does not have to be considered during requirements engineering.

Concretion and shift of the context boundary

At the beginning of the requirements engineering process, frequently only part of the environment as well as single specific relationships between the environment and the system to be developed are known. In the course of requirements engineering, it is necessary to concretize the boundary between system context and irrelevant environment by analyzing relevant aspects within the environment with regard to their relationships to the system. Besides the system boundary, the context boundary typically also shifts during requirements engineering. For instance, it may be possible that a law directive that was considered to be relevant for the system to be developed no longer impacts the system or is no longer considered relevant. The system context is therefore reduced (① in figure 2-4). If a new law directive is identified that influences the system, the system context is extended accordingly (② in figure 2-4).

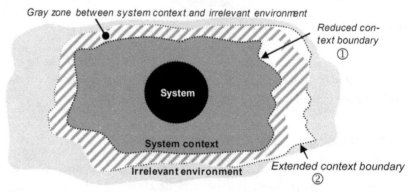

Figure 2-4 *Gray zone between system context and irrelevant environment*

Gray zone between system context and irrelevant environment

Since the context boundary separates the system context from those parts of reality that are irrelevant to the system, a complete and precise definition of the context boundary for complex systems is virtually impossible. In addition, it may not be possible to clarify for single aspects of the environment whether they influence the system to be developed or are influenced by it or not. These two observations are the reason for the existence of a gray zone with regard to the context boundary (see figure 2-4).

This gray zone therefore comprises identified aspects of the environment for which it is unclear whether they have a relation to the system or not. In contrast to the gray zone between the system and the system context that must be resolved in the course of requirements engineering, it is not necessary to resolve the gray zone between the system context and the irrelevant environment entirely.

Resolving and shifting of the gray zone

2.3   Documenting the System Context

In order to document the system context (especially the system and context boundaries), "use case" diagrams [Jacobson et al. 1992] (see sections 4.2.3 and 6.3.1) or "data flow" diagrams [DeMarco 1978] (see section 6.6.1) are often used. When the context is modeled with data flow diagrams, sources and sinks in the environment of the system that represent the source or destination of data flows (or flows of material, energy, money, etc.) are modeled. In use case diagrams, actors (such as people or other systems) in the system environment and their usage relationships to the system are modeled. To model the system context, UML class diagrams [OMG 2007] (see section 6.5.2) may also be used. In order to document the system context of a system as thoroughly as possible, typically several documentation forms are used.

2.4   Summary

The system context is the part of the reality that influences the system to be developed and thus also influences the requirements for the system. In order to be able to elicit the requirements for the system to be developed, it is necessary to define the boundary of the system to the system context and the boundary of the system context to the irrelevant environment first. When the system boundaries are defined, the scope of the system is determined. The scope comprises those aspects that can be changed and designed during system development. At the same time, it is also defined which aspects belong to the environment and thus cannot be altered during development and may provide constraints for the system to be developed.

The context boundary separates the part of the environment that influences the requirements for the system to be developed from that part that does not influence the requirements. Typical aspects within the system context are stakeholders (e.g., the users of the system) and documents (e.g., standards that have to be considered) as well as other systems that, for instance, interact with the system to be developed. Defining the system and context boundaries successfully is the foundation for a systematic elicitation of requirements for the system to be developed.

3 Eliciting Requirements

A core activity of requirements engineering is the elicitation of requirements for the system to be developed. The basis for requirements elicitation is the knowledge that has been gained during requirements engineering about the system context of the system to be developed, which comprises the requirements sources that are to be analyzed and queried.

3.1 Requirements Sources

There are three different kinds of requirements sources:

Three types of requirements sources

- *Stakeholders* (see section 1.1.2) are people or organizations that (directly or indirectly) influence the requirements of a system. Examples of stakeholders are users of the system, operators of the system, developers, architects, customers, and testers.
- *Documents* often contain important information that can provide requirements. Examples of documents are universal documents, such as standards and legal documents, as well as domain- or organization-specific documents, such as requirements documents and error reports of legacy systems.
- *Systems in operation* can be legacy or predecessor systems as well as competing systems. By giving the stakeholders a chance to try the system out, they can gain an impression of the current system and can request extensions or changes based on their impressions.

3.1.1 Stakeholders and Their Significance

Identifying the relevant stakeholders is a central task of requirements engineering [Glinz and Wieringa 2007]. For the requirements engineer, stakeholders are important sources of requirements for the system (see section 1.1.2). It is the task of the requirements engineer to gather,

Significance of stakeholders

document, and consolidate the partially conflicting goals and requirements of different stakeholders [Potts et al. 1994] (see chapter 8).

Consequences of unconsidered stakeholders

If stakeholders are not identified or not considered, it may result in significant negative repercussions for the project progress because requirements may remain undetected. At the latest, these overlooked requirements will enter the picture in the form of change requests during system operation. Fixing these issues retroactively causes high additional costs. Therefore, it is essential to identify all stakeholders and integrate them into the elicitation procedures.

Stakeholder lists provide overview.

An auxiliary technique for stakeholder identification is maintaining checklists. This allows for systematic and targeted elicitation of relevant stakeholders. If the stakeholder list is updated too late or incompletely, the result may be that important aspects of the system remain undetected, that the project goal is missed, or that significant additional costs arise from fixing issues. The starting point for stakeholder elicitation is often suggestions of relevant stakeholders that are made by management or by domain experts, for example. On the basis of these suggestions, relevant stakeholders can be identified.

3.1.2   Handling Stakeholders in the Project

Managing stakeholders

It can often be observed in practice that a lot of stakeholders are involved in complex and "difficult" projects. Due to limited resources, the stakeholders that are the most suitable for requirements elicitation must be carefully selected. To document the stakeholders in the development process, it makes sense to use tables and spreadsheets that contain (at least) the following data: name, function (role), additional personal and contact data, temporal and spatial availability during the project progress, relevance of the stakeholder, area and extent of expertise of the stakeholder, and the stakeholder's goals and interests regarding the project.

Making collaborators out of the affected

Handling stakeholders also means continuously exchanging information: Periodic status updates and continuous involvement of the stakeholders assist the requirements engineer in turning people previously simply affected by the project (i.e., principally affected stakeholders) into collaborators (i.e., well-integrated, jointly responsible stakeholders).

Stakeholders that are not given enough attention by the requirements engineer might be overly critical toward the project. In addition, some stakeholders may show a lack of motivation because they are sufficiently satisfied with the legacy system, are afraid of change, or are negatively biased due to previous projects. It's the requirements engineer's task to support the project manager in convincing all stakeholders of the benefit of the project. To avoid misunderstandings and disputes regarding competence, it is useful to formally agree on the tasks, responsibilities, and managerial authority as well as to determine individual goals, communication paths, and feedback loops that can be used by the stakeholders. Depending on the culture of the organization, this agreement and determination can be done verbally (i.e., by "shaking hands") or, more formally, by means of written documentation. The individual agreements should be signed off by the managers.

Individual "contracts" with the stakeholders

A number of obligations and privileges result from the agreement with the stakeholders.

Obligations and privileges of the stakeholders

The requirements engineer

- speaks the language of the stakeholders,
- becomes thoroughly familiar with the application domain,
- creates a requirements document,
- is able to get work results across (e.g., by means of diagrams and graphs),
- maintains a respectful relationship with any stakeholder,
- presents her ideas and alternatives as well as their realizations,
- allows stakeholders to demand properties that make the system user-friendly and simple,
- ensures that the system satisfies the functional and qualitative demands of the stakeholders.

The stakeholders

- introduce the requirements engineer to the application domain,
- supply the requirements engineer with requirements,
- document requirements assiduously,
- make timely decisions,
- respect the requirements engineer's estimates of costs and feasibility,
- prioritize requirements,
- inspect the requirements that the requirements engineer documents, such as prototypes, etc.,

- communicate changes in requirements immediately,
- adhere to the predetermined change process,
- respect the requirements engineering process that has been instated.

Elicitation techniques determine communication and process.

In addition, the requirements engineer plans and organizes the communication paths as well as drafts a structured schedule for the requirements engineering activities that are to be performed in collaboration with the stakeholders. This organization and the type of communication are significantly influenced by the elicitation techniques that can be used during requirements engineering.

3.2   Requirements Categorization According to the Kano Model

Influence of the requirements on satisfaction

Knowing the importance of a requirement for the satisfaction of the stakeholders is very helpful for requirements elicitation. Along with the respective properties of a product that determine the satisfaction, the satisfaction is classified into the following three categories [Kano et al. 1984]:

- *Dissatisfiers* are properties of the system that are self-evident and taken for granted (subconscious knowledge).
- *Satisfiers* are explicitly demanded system properties (conscious knowledge).
- *Delighters* are system properties that the stakeholder does not know or expect and discovers only while using the system—a pleasant and useful surprise (unconscious knowledge).

As time goes by, delighters turn into satisfiers and dissatisfiers as the user becomes accustomed to the properties of the system. When eliciting requirements, all three categories must be considered.

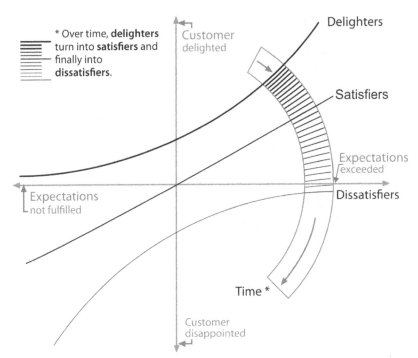

Figure 3-1 *Graphical representation of the Kano model*

Dissatisfiers (subconscious requirements) must be fulfilled by the system   *Dissatisfiers*
in any case. Otherwise, stakeholders will be disappointed and dissatisfied.
Completely fulfilled dissatisfiers do not generate a positive disposition but
merely help to avoid massive discontent. Dissatisfiers are dominantly
influenced by existing systems. Therefore, observation and document-centric techniques are especially well suited for the elicitation of these factors.

Satisfiers (conscious requirements) are properties that are consciously   *Satisfiers*
known to the stakeholders and explicitly demanded. When these properties are fulfilled, stakeholders are content and satisfied, which is desirable.
If some demanded properties are missing, the stakeholders probably will
not accept the product. Their satisfaction decreases with each missing satisfier. Satisfiers can be elicited well using survey techniques.

Delighters (unconscious requirements) are properties of a system   *Delighters*
whose value is recognized only when the stakeholder can try out the system for herself or the requirements engineer proposes them. Creativity
techniques are best suited to elicit delighters.

3.3 Elicitation Techniques

The main goal of all elicitation techniques is in supporting the requirements engineer in ascertaining the knowledge and requirements of the stakeholders. How and when a technique can be applied depends on the given conditions. Applying the technique consciously and in a fashion appropriate to the situation at hand allows for tailoring the requirements elicitation process which takes into account project constraints so that requirements may be elicited as completely and comprehensibly as possible.

3.3.1 Types of Elicitation Techniques

Elicitation techniques serve the purpose of identifying the conscious, unconscious, and subconscious stakeholder requirements. However, there is no universal method to elicit these requirements [Hickey and Davis 2003]. Every project has individual constraints and individual characteristics and is by and large unique, but there are always elicitation techniques that are compatible with the project. The most important influencing factors when choosing the appropriate elicitation techniques are as follows:

- the distinction between conscious, unconscious, and subconscious requirements that are to be elicited
- the time and budget constraints, as well as the availability of the stakeholders
- the experience of the requirements engineer with a particular elicitation technique
- the chances and risks of the project

The first important step when choosing a suitable elicitation technique is to perform an analysis of constraints critical to the project, i.e., identifying so-called risk factors. Mostly, these result from human, organizational, and professional influences, as illustrated in the following passages.

During the requirements elicitation phase, which is heavily influenced by the stakeholders, good communication is essential. In order to assure high-quality communication between the requirements engineer and stakeholders, it is important to determine the type of requirement, the desired level of detail, and the experience of the requirements engineer and the interviewees with different elicitation techniques.

Social, group-dynamic, and cognitive capabilities of the stakeholders also influence the choice of suitable elicitation techniques significantly.

Another influence factor is whether the elicited knowledge is explicit (consciously known) by each individual stakeholder or if it is implicit or unconscious (i.e., covert).

Organizational risk factors the project faces need to be investigated as well. Among other things, this comprises the distinction between fixed price contracts and service contracts, whether the system to be built is a new development or an extension of a legacy system, and spatial and temporal availability of the stakeholders.

Organizational influences

In addition, it is necessary to consider the operational content of the requirements. If the system is very complex, it is advisable to employ a structuring approach during elicitation in order to deconstruct the operational contents into understandable parts.

Operational influences of the content

Another influencing factor on the choice of elicitation techniques is the desired level of detail of the requirements. Abstract requirements can be elicited rather well using creativity techniques. With the stakeholders, a vision of the system or its important properties can be created or collected. Inquisitive (survey) techniques or observational techniques can aid in eliciting requirements of a medium level of detail [Robertson 2002]. Finely detailed requirements can be elicited well by making use of document-centric techniques, i.e., techniques that use existing documents because information up to an arbitrary level of detail can be extracted from these.

Combine techniques with regard to your particular situation to lower risks.

It is advisable to combine different techniques because this minimizes many of the risks inherent to the project. Weaknesses and pitfalls of a particular technique can be balanced out through the use of another technique whose strong points lie where the first technique may have deficits.

3.3.2   Survey Techniques

Survey techniques aim at eliciting as precise and unbiased statements as possible from stakeholders regarding their requirements. All survey techniques assume that the respondent is capable of explicitly expressing his or her knowledge and that he or she is committed to investing time and effort for the elicitation. Survey techniques are usually driven by the requirements engineer because she asks the questions. This, however, might result in the fact that stakeholder concerns are forgotten, superseded, or disregarded.

Eliciting explicit knowledge

▧ During an *interview*, the requirements engineer asks predetermined questions to one or more stakeholders and documents the answers. Questions that arise during the conversation can be discussed immedi-

Interview

ately, and the requirements engineer may uncover subconscious requirements through clever questions. Interviews can be employed during the entire development phase of the system. An experienced interviewer individually controls the course of the conversation, completely commits herself to each stakeholder, inquires about specific aspects, and thus ensures the completeness of the answers. The most prominent disadvantage of this elicitation technique is that it is very time-consuming.

Questionnaire

- *Questionnaire:* Making use of open and/or closed questions (e.g., multiple choice questions) is another way of eliciting requirements from stakeholders. If there are a large number of participants that must be surveyed, an online questionnaire is a viable option. Questionnaires can elicit a magnitude of information in a short amount of time and at low costs. As long as answers are predetermined, even stakeholders that are not able to explicitly express their knowledge can deliver an assessment. A disadvantage of using a questionnaire is that it can be only employed to gather requirements the requirements engineer already knows or conjectures. Creating a proper questionnaire is often tricky and time-consuming and requires thorough knowledge of the domain in question and the psychological guidelines for creating questionnaires. In addition, as opposed to interviews, questionnaires do not provide immediate feedback between the surveyor and the surveyed, so it becomes apparent that questions were forgotten or badly formulated only once the questionnaires have been evaluated.

3.3.3 Creativity Techniques

Establishing innovations

Creativity techniques serve the purpose of developing innovative requirements, delineating an initial vision of the system, and eliciting excitement factors. Creativity techniques are usually not well suited for establishing fine-grained requirements about the system behavior. The following creativity techniques are commonly used [Maiden and Gizikis 2001]:

Brainstorming

- During *brainstorming*, ideas are collected within a certain time frame, usually in groups of 5 to 10 people. The ideas are documented by a moderator without discussing, judging, or commenting on them at first. Participants use ideas of other participants to develop new original ideas or to modify existing ideas. After that, the collected ideas are subjected to a thorough analysis. This technique is especially effective when a large number of people of different stakeholder groups are involved. Among the advantages of this technique is that a large number of ideas can be collected in a short amount of time and multiple people can expand on these ideas collaboratively. The unbiased collection of these ideas allows new solutions to pop up. Brainstorming is usually less effective when the dynamics of the group are muddled or when participants with very varied levels of dominance are involved. For such situations, other creativity techniques may be better suited, e.g., the 6-3-5 method (six participants, three ideas each, fivefold hand-off of the ideas) [Rohrbach 1969] or the brainwriting method.

- *Brainstorming paradox* is a modification of regular brainstorming in that events that must not occur are collected. Afterward, the group develops measures to prevent the events collected earlier from happening. Through this process, participants often realize which actions may entail negative results. With this method, risks can be identified early on and countermeasures can be developed. Advantages and disadvantages of this technique are identical to those of classic brainstorming.

  Brainstorming paradox

- *Change of perspective:* Among the techniques that employ a change of perspective (adopting different extreme standpoints), the most common technique is the so-called Six Thinking Hats [DeBono 2006]. Each of the six hats represents a particular perspective that is in turn adopted by each of the participants. The resulting solutions approach the problem from different standpoints. That way, even stakeholders that are very convinced of their own opinion are persuaded to adopt a different standpoint. This technique is extraordinarily beneficial when stakeholders can only express their knowledge in a biased manner or are harshly constricted to their opinions. On the other hand, this technique cannot be applied if the requirements require a fine-grained level of detail because this would render the technique very laborious.

  Change of perspective

- *Analogy techniques (bionics/bisociations):* In bionics, problems that the project faces are mapped to an analogous situation occurring in nature, and the solutions nature provides are sought and then mapped back to the project. In bisociation, the analogies need not originate in nature. These techniques assume that each participant is capable of analogous thinking, that a lot of time is available, and that the participants have an in-depth knowledge of the domain with which an analogy will be drawn. Analogy techniques can be applied covertly or in the open. When this technique is applied covertly, the participants are only told the analogy. The requirements engineer is then responsible

  Analogy technique

for mapping the results onto the real problem space. When this technique is applied in the open, the stakeholders know the real problem space as well as the analogy.

3.3.4   Document-centric Techniques

Document-centric techniques reuse solutions and experiences made with existing systems. When a legacy system is replaced, this technique ensures that the entire functionality of the legacy system can be identified. Document-centric techniques should be combined with other elicitation techniques so that the validity of the elicited requirements can be determined and new requirements for the new system can be identified.

System archaeology

System archaeology is a technique that extracts information required to build a new system from the documentation or implementation (code) of a legacy system or a competitor's system. The technique is often applied when explicit knowledge about the system logic has been lost partially or entirely. By analyzing existing code, the requirements engineer ensures that none of the functionalities of the legacy system will be overlooked and the system logic of the legacy system is elicited anew. This method leads to a large amount of very detailed requirements and is very laborious. However, system archaeology is the only technique that can ensure that all functionalities of the legacy system will be implemented in the new system. When it becomes obviously apparent that the legacy system and the new system differ in functionality, additional elicitation techniques, e.g., creativity techniques, must be applied early on.

Perspective-based reading

Perspective-based reading (see section 7.5.4) is applied when documents need to be read with a particular perspective in mind, e.g., the perspective of the implementer or the tester. Aspects that are contained in the document but do not pertain to the current perspective are ignored. This allows for an analysis that is strictly focused on particular parts of the existing documentation. This way, detailed, technology-related or implementation-related aspects can be separated from essential operational aspects that are relevant for the successor system.

Reuse

Reuse: Requirements that have been previously compiled and brought up to a certain quality standard can be reused. In order to do that, the requirements are stored in a database, for instance, and kept available at the required level of detail for reuse. Through reuse, the costs involved with the elicitation procedures can be significantly reduced.

3.3.5   Observation Techniques

When domain specialists are unable to spend the time needed to share their expertise with the requirements engineer, or are unable to express and denote their knowledge, observation techniques are helpful. During observation, the requirements engineer observes the stakeholders while they go about their work. The requirements engineer documents all steps and thus elicits the processes the system must support as well as potential mistakes, risks, and open questions. All those are potential requirements that need to be formulated. The stakeholders can actively demonstrate their knowledge in using the application or can remain passive, with the requirements engineer merely observing. The requirements engineer ought to question the observed processes so that the situation as it should be can be established. Otherwise, she is at risk of documenting outdated technological decisions and suboptimal processes (i.e., the situation as is and not as it should be). As the requirements engineer is an external observer, her chances of identifying inefficient processes are good and she can then suggest better solutions. She is farther removed from the processes than the stakeholders, who frequently repeat work steps without questioning them critically. Observation techniques are well suited to elicit detailed requirements and dissatisfiers because the requirements engineer can recognize dissatisfiers thought of as self-evident or only subconsciously known by the stakeholders. In addition, the requirements engineer becomes very familiar with the domain language, which simplifies further elicitation. Satisfiers can only be observed if they have been implemented in the legacy system or are actively employed in the current processes. As a result, this technique is not suited for the development of new processes. During system development, field observations and apprenticing are especially well suited as elicitation techniques.

Question observations and optimize processes.

- *Field observation:* The requirements engineer is on location with the specialist or the users of the system and observes and documents the processes and operational procedures that they carry out. Using these observations, she formulates the requirements. Often, this can be further aided by audio and video recordings. This technique is well suited for operational procedures that are difficult to express verbally, but it can only be applied if the procedures are visible physically.

Field observation

- With *apprenticing*, the requirements engineer must actively learn and perform the procedures of the stakeholders. Just like an apprentice, the requirements engineer is encouraged to question unclear and complex

Apprenticing

operational procedures so that she may gather domain experience. Thereby, she can experience requirements that the stakeholders take for granted and therefore cannot elucidate. Another advantage is that the typical balance of power between the requirements engineer and the respective specialist is reversed because the stakeholder now adopts the role of the "master" that has the knowledge the apprentice is yet lacking.

3.3.6   Support Techniques

Support techniques serve as an addition to the elicitation techniques and try to balance out the weaknesses and pitfalls of the chosen elicitation technique.

Mind mapping ▪ In *mind mapping,* a graphical representation of the refined relationships and interdependencies between terms is created. Mind mapping is often used as a supporting technique for brainstorming or brainstorming paradox.

Workshops ▪ During a joint meeting, the requirements engineer and the stakeholders elaborate the goals (or details of a certain functionality) of the system. For example, the necessary user interfaces of the system can be designed in a *workshop* [Gottesdiener 2002].

CRC cards ▪ With the CRC technique (CRC stands for *Class Responsibility Collaboration*), context aspects and their respective attributes and properties are denoted on index cards. Requirements are then formulated using these cards.

Audio and video recordings ▪ *Audio and video recordings* are very well suited to elicit requirements when stakeholders are not always available, when budget is tight, or when the system is highly critical. Especially during field observations, audio and video recordings can help capture fast-paced processes. The disadvantage of this technique is that stakeholders often feel supervised when they are being recorded and as a result might deliver biased statements or, in extreme cases, might even refuse to cooperate.

Modeling action sequences ▪ *Use case modeling:* Use cases document the external view of the system to be developed. A use case has a trigger event, which triggers the use case and an expected result, or outcome of the use case. Every use case is a functionality that must be supported by the system to be developed (see section 6.3).

Prototypes for illustration ▪ *Prototypes* are well suited to question established requirements and to elicit requirements in situations where stakeholders have only a vague understanding of what is to be developed. Potential consequences of new or changed requirements can be identified easier. For example, user interface prototypes are frequently used in practice to find additional functional requirements.

3.4 Summary

Requirements elicitation is a core activity in requirements engineering. Aside from documents and legacy systems, stakeholders are the main sources for requirements. It is important to initially agree upon mutual rights and responsibilities of the stakeholders and the requirements engineer in order to facilitate communication and cooperation and to successfully integrate the stakeholders into the elicitation process. The choice of the right elicitation technique for the respective project is made by the requirements engineer based on the given cultural, organizational, and domain-specific constraints.

4 Documenting Requirements

In requirements engineering, information that has been established or worked out during different activities must be documented. Among this information are, for example, protocols of interviews and reports of validation or agreement activities, but also change requests. The main and most important documentation task in requirements engineering, though, is to document the requirements for the system in a suitable manner.

4.1 Document Design

A documentation technique is any kind of more or less formal depiction that eases communication between stakeholders and increases the quality of the documented requirements. In principle, any kind of documentation technique can be used to document the requirements, let it be natural language-based documentation by means of prose, more structured natural language-based text, or more formal techniques such as state diagrams.

Definition 4-1: *Requirements Document / Requirements Specification*

A requirements specification is a systematically represented collection of requirements, typically for a system or component, that satisfies given criteria.

During the life cycle of a requirements document, many people are trusted with the documentation. During communication, the documentation has a goal-oriented and supporting role. The main reasons for documenting requirements are as follows:

Reasons for the documentation

- *Requirements are the basis of the system development.* Requirements of any kind influence the analysis, design, implementation, and test phases directly and indirectly. The quality of a requirement or of a requirements document has a strong impact on the progress of the project and therefore on its success.

Central role of requirements

Legal relevance   ▦ *Requirements have a legal relevance.* Requirements are legally binding for the contractor and the client, and the client can sue for their fulfillment. Documenting the requirements can help to quickly overcome legal conflicts between two or more parties.

Complexity   ▦ *Requirements documents are complex.* Systems that possess thousands of requirements that in turn have complex interdependencies on multiple layers are not unheard of in practice. Without suitable documentation, keeping on top of things can become very difficult for anyone involved.

Accessibility   ▦ *Requirements must be accessible to all involved parties.* Projects undergo certain "development" as time goes by—with regard to the subject as well as the staff. When requirements can be permanently accessed, uncertainty and obscurities can be avoided and staff that has recently joined the project can quickly get up to speed.

Another argument for a good documentation, supportive of the project, is that employees almost never share the same understanding of a subject matter. Therefore, requirements should be documented in a way that they meet the quality demands of all involved.

4.2   Types of Documentation

Requirements for a system can be documented in three different perspectives. In practice, natural language as well as conceptual models are used to this end, or oftentimes, an advantageous combination of both is employed.

4.2.1   The Three Perspectives of Requirements

Requirements for a system can be documented in three different perspectives onto the system to be developed:

Data perspective   ▦ *Data perspective:* In the data perspective, a static-structural perspective on the requirements of the system is adopted. For example, the structure of input and output data as well as static-structural aspects of usage and dependency relations of the system and the system context can be documented (e.g., the services of an external system).

Functional perspective   ▦ *Functional perspective:* The functional perspective documents which information (data) is received from the system context and manipulated by the system or one of its functions. This perspective also documents which data flows back into the system context. The order in which functions processing the input data are executed is also documented.

- *Behavioral perspective:* In the behavioral perspective, information about the system and how it is embedded into the system context is documented in a state-oriented manner. This is done by documenting the reactions of the system upon events in the system context, the conditions that warrant a state transition, and the effects that the system shall have on its environment (e.g., effects of the system analyzed that represent events in the system context of a different system).

Behavioral perspective

4.2.2   Requirements Documentation using Natural Language

Natural language, particularly prose, is the most commonly applied documentation form for requirements in practice. In contrast to other documentation forms, prose has a striking advantage: No stakeholder has to learn a new notation. In addition, language can be used for miscellaneous purposes—the requirements engineer can use natural language to express any kind of requirement.

Advantages of using natural language

Natural-language-based documentation is well suited to document requirements in any of the three perspectives. However, natural language can allow requirements to be ambiguous, and requirements of different types and perspectives are in danger of being unintentionally mixed up during documentation. In that case, it is difficult to isolate information pertaining to a certain perspective amidst all of the requirements in natural language.

Disadvantages of using natural language

4.2.3   Requirements Documentation using Conceptual Models

In contrast to natural language, the different types of conceptual models cannot be used universally. When documenting requirements by means of models, special modeling languages must be used that pertain to the appropriate perspective. Assuming the modeling language selected for a documentation task is applied correctly, its use constructively guarantees that the models created depict information pertaining to the respective perspective only. The models depict the documented requirements much more compactly and they therefore are easier for a trained reader to understand than is natural language. In addition, conceptual models offer a decreased degree of ambiguity (i.e., fewer ways to be interpreted) than natural language due to their higher degree of formality. However, using conceptual modeling languages for requirements documentation requires specific knowledge of modeling. The following list includes short descriptions of the most important diagrams discussed in chapter 6.

Overview of system functions

- *Use case diagram:* A use case diagram allows you to gain a quick overview of the functionalities of the specified system. A use case describes which functions are offered to the user by the system and how these functions relate to other external interacting entities. However, use cases do not describe the responsibilities that the functions have in detail (see section 6.3).

Structural data modeling and structuring of terms

- *Class diagram:* Among other things, class diagrams are used in requirements engineering to document requirements with regard to the static structure of data, to document static-structural dependencies between the system and the system context, or to document complex domain terms in a structured manner (see section 6.5.2).

Sequence modeling

- *Activity diagram:* Using activity diagrams, business processes, or sequence-oriented dependencies of the system in regard to processes within the system context can be documented. Activity diagrams are also well suited to model the sequential character of use cases or to model a detailed specification of the interaction of functions that process data (see section 6.6.3).

Event-driven behavior

- *State diagram:* State diagrams are used in requirements engineering to document event-driven behavior of a system. The focus of this type of model is on the individual states the system can be in, events and their respective conditions that trigger a state transition, and effects of the system in its environment.

4.2.4   Hybrid Requirements Documents

Combined use of documentation types

Requirements documents first and foremost contain requirements. In addition, in many situations it is sensible to document decisions, important explanations, and other relevant information as well. Depending on the target audience of the document, the perspective on the system, and the documented knowledge, suitable documentation types are selected. Typically, documents contain a combination of natural language and conceptual models. The combination allows the disadvantages of both documentation types to be decreased by means of the strengths of the other documentation type, and combining documentation types exploits the advantages of both. For instance, models can be amended or complemented by natural language comments and natural language requirements and natural language glossaries can be summarized and their dependencies can be depicted clearly by making use of models.

4.3 Document Structures

Requirements documents contain a magnitude of different information. These must be well structured for the reader. In order to do that, one can make use of standardized document structures or individually define a custom document structure.

Influence of the requirements on satisfaction

4.3.1 Standardized Document Structures

Standard outlines offer a predefined structure, i.e., predefined stereotypes according to which the information can be classified. By using standard outlines, a rough structure along with a short description of the content of the main sections is predetermined. Using standard outlines has the following advantages:

Adaptation of existing standard outlines

- Standard outlines simplify incorporating new staff members.
- Standard outlines allow for quickly finding desired contents.
- Standard outlines allow for selective reading and validation of requirements documents.
- Standard outlines allow for automatic verification of requirements documents (e.g., with regard to completeness).
- Standard outlines allow for simplified reuse of the contents of requirements documents.

It must be noted that these structures must be tailored with regard to the specific project properties to meet the respective constraints. In the following paragraphs, three of the most widely used standardized document structures are introduced.

The *Rational Unified Process (RUP)* [Kruchten 2001]is usually used for software systems that are developed using object-oriented methods. The client creates a *business model* that contains different artifacts from the business environment (e.g., business rules, business use cases, business goals), which serve as the basis for requirements of the system over the course of development. The contractor uses the structures of the *software*

Rational Unified Process

requirements specification (SRS) to document all software requirements. These structures are closely related to the ISO/IEC/IEEE standard 29148:2011, as described next.

The ISO/IEC/IEEE standard 29148:2011 [ISO/IEC/IEEE 29148:2011] contains an outline designed for the documentation of software requirements (software requirements specification). The standard structure suggests dividing the requirements document into five parts with regard to their subject matter:

- A chapter with introductory information (e.g., system goal, system bounding) and a general description of the software (e.g., perspective of the system, properties of future users)
- A chapter with a listing of all documents that are referenced in the specification
- A chapter for specific requirements (e.g., functional requirements, performance, interfaces)
- A chapter with all planned measures for verification
- Appendices (e.g., information about assumptions that were made, identified dependencies)

The *V-Model* [V-Modell 2004] of the German Federal Ministry of the Interior (BMI) defines different structures, depending on the creator of the requirements document:

- The *Customer Requirements Specification*, known in the German original as Lastenheft, is created by the customer and describes all of the demands to the contractor regarding the subject of the contract, i.e., deliveries and services. In addition, in many cases, demands of the users, including all constraints to the system and the development process, are documented. Therefore, the Customer Requirements Specification usually describes *what* is made *for what*.
- The *System Requirements Specification*, known in the German original as Pflichtenheft, is based on the Customer Requirements Specification and contains the implementation suggestions that the contractor has elaborated. Therefore, the System Requirements Specification is a refinement of the requirements and constraints of the Customer Requirements Specification.

4.3.2   Customized Standard Contents

As described in section 4.3.1, standardized document structures are adapted with regard to the specific project conditions. The following issues should be addressed by any chosen structure.

The minimum content

Introduction

The introduction contains information about the entire document. This information allows gaining a quick overview of the system.

- *Purpose:* This section discusses why the document was created and who the target audience for the requirements document is.
- *System coverage:* This part consists of the system to be developed. It indicates system name and the principle goals and advantages that arise from introducing the system.
- *Stakeholder:* This section contains a list of stakeholders and their relevant information (see section 3.1.1).
- *Definitions, Acronyms, and Abbreviations:*[1] In this section, the terms used in the document are defined so that they can be used consistently throughout the document.
- *References:*[2] All documents that are referenced by the requirements document are listed herein.
- *Overview:* At the end of the introductory chapter, the content and structure of the following sections of the requirements document should be explained briefly.

General Overview

In this section, additional information is documented that increases the understandability of the requirements. In contrast to the introduction, this is merely operational information that does not pertain to administration, management, or organizational aspects of the requirements document.

- *System environment:* The embedding of the system into the environment is of key concern in this paragraph. The results of your definition of the system boundary and context boundary can be found herein.
- *Architecture description:* In this section, the operational interfaces of the system (e.g., user interfaces, hardware and software interfaces, and

---

1.   This section can also be treated as an appendix to the document.
2.   This section can also be treated as an appendix to the document.

communication interfaces) are documented. In addition, further information, e.g., regarding storage limitations, is also discussed.

- *System functionality:* This section contains the coarse functionalities and tasks of the system. This can be documented, for example, using a use case diagram.
- *User and target audience:* The different users of the system that make up the target audience are listed.
- *Constraints:* In this section, all conditions ought to be listed that have not been documented thus far and might hinder the requirements engineering.
- *Assumptions:* Decisions, such as not implementing certain aspects of the system due to budgeting reasons, or other general assumptions about the system context that the requirements are based upon are documented here.

Requirements

This part contains functional requirements as well as quality requirements.

Appendices

In the appendices, additional information that completes the document can be documented. For example, the appendices can include additional documents regarding the user characteristics, standards, conventions, or background information regarding the requirements document.

Index

The index typically contains a table of contents (i.e., a structure of the chapters) and an index directory. In highly dynamic requirements documents, this may be a highly critical section that must be kept up-to-date.

4.4 Using Requirements Documents

Requirements documents as the basis for development

Over the course of the project, requirements documents serve as the basis for different tasks:

- *Planning:* Based on the requirements document, concrete work packages and milestones for the implementation of the system can be defined.

- *Architectural design:* The detailed documented requirements (along with constraints) serve as the basis for the design of the system architecture.
- *Implementation:* Based on the architectural design, the system is implemented by making use of the requirements.
- *Test:* On the basis of requirements that have been documented in the requirements document, test cases can be developed that can be used for system validation later on.
- *Change management:* When requirements change, the requirements document can serve as the basis to analyze the extent to which other parts of the system are influenced. The change effort can thus be estimated.
- *System usage and system maintenance:* After the system is developed, the requirements document is used for maintenance and support. This way, the requirements document can be used to analyze concrete defects and shortcomings that surface during system use. For example, one can deduct if a defect is a result of using the system incorrectly, a result of an error in requirements, or a result of an error in implementation.
- *Contract management:* The requirements document is the prime subject of a contract between a client and a contractor in many cases.

4.5   Quality Criteria for Requirements Documents

To become a basis for the subsequent processes, the requirements document must meet certain quality criteria. According to the ISO/IEC/IEEE standard 29148:2011 [ISO/IEC/IEEE 29148:2011], a requirements document shall be complete and consistent. Moreover, a requirements document shall support readability by offering a clear structure, reasonable scope, and traceability. Overall, a requirements document shall fulfil the following quality criteria:

- Unambiguity and consistency
- Clear structure
- Modifiability and extendibility
- Completeness
- Traceability

4.5.1   Unambiguity and Consistency

Quality of individual requirements is a prerequisite.

Requirements documents can be consistent and unambiguous only when the individual requirements are consistent and unambiguous. In addition, it must be guaranteed that individual requirements do not contradict one another. To achieve this, it is advisable to make use of conceptual models (see chapter 6). Another aspect of unambiguity pertains to the unique identification of a requirements document or a requirement among the set of all requirements documents or requirements in a development project (see section 8.5).

4.5.2   Clear Structure

Allows for selective reading

In order to guarantee that the requirements document is readable by any stakeholder, it should be appropriately comprehensive and clearly structured. Unfortunately, no clear-cut suggestions can be made regarding the appropriate comprehensiveness of a requirements document. A very comprehensive requirements document with a good structure can be just as appropriate as a less comprehensive document because a clear structure will allow the reader to skip parts that are not relevant to him. An unstructured or badly structured requirements document of the same high level of comprehensiveness would not be appropriate because the document must be read in its entirety in order for a stakeholder to be able to identify parts that are relevant to her. A good starting point is the standard structures described in section 4.3.1.

4.5.3   Modifiability and Extendibility

Content and structure should support changeability.

Requirements documents must be easy to extend. There are always requirements that are changed, altered, added, or removed as a project progresses. As a result, the structure of requirements documents should be easy to modify and extend. The requirements documents of a project should be subject to the project's version control management.

4.5.4   Completeness

Two types of completeness in requirements documents

Requirements documents must be complete, i.e., they must contain all relevant requirements (and required additional information), and each requirement must be documented completely.[3] All possible inputs, influential factors, and required reactions of the system must be described for each desired system function. This comprises describing error and exception cases in particular. Also, quality requirements, such as requirements pertaining to reaction times or availability and usability of the system, must be noted.

Formal factors also contribute to completeness. Graphs, diagrams, and tables should be appropriately labeled. Another important aspect is that consistent reference and index directories must exist. Also, definitions and norm reference that denote specific terms must be included in any requirements document. The comprehensiveness of a requirements document is a challenge during requirements engineering. Often, a compromise must be found between the time resources available and the completeness of the requirements documents.

Evidence, reference, and sources are formal necessities.

4.5.5   Traceability

An important quality criterion is traceability of relationships between requirements documents and other documents (e.g., business process model, test plans, or design plans). These documents could have been created in previous development phases, in subsequent development phases, or concurrently with the requirements documents. Among other things, traceability supports change management (see section 8.4).

Relationship to other development documents

4.6   Quality Criteria for Requirements

Each documented requirement should fulfil the following quality criteria:

Quality criteria for single document requirements

- *Agreed*: A requirement is agreed upon if it is correct and necessary in the opinion of all stakeholders.
- *Unambiguous*: [ISO/IEC/IEEE 29148:2011] A requirement that is unambiguously documented can be understood in only one way. It must not be possible to interpret the requirement in a different way. All readers of the requirement must arrive at the same understanding of the requirement.
- *Necessary*: [ISO/IEC/IEEE 29148:2011] A documented requirement must represent the facts and conditions of the system context in a way

---

3.   Strictly speaking, this statement holds true only for the requirements document of the next system release (see section 8.5.3).

that it is valid with regard to the actualities of the system context. These actualities may be the different stakeholders' ideas, relevant standards, or interfaces to external systems.

- *Consistent*: [ISO/IEC/IEEE 29148:2011] Requirements must be consistent with regard to all other requirements, i.e., the requirements must not contradict one another, regardless of their level of detail or documentation type. In addition, a requirement must be formulated in a way that allows for consistency with itself, i.e., the requirement may not contradict itself.

- *Verifiable*: [ISO/IEC/IEEE 29148:2011] A requirement must be described in a way that allows for verification. That means that tests or measurements can be carried out that provide evidence of the functionality demanded by the requirement.

- *Feasible*: [ISO/IEC/IEEE 29148:2011] It must be possible to implement each requirement given the organizational, legal, technical, or financial constraints. This means that a member of the development team ought to be involved in rating the goals and requirements so that he can show the technical limits of the implementation of a particular requirement. In addition, the costs for the implementation must be incorporated into the rating. Occasionally, stakeholders withdraw a requirement if the costs for its realization become apparent.

- *Traceable*: [ISO/IEC/IEEE 29148:2011] A requirement is traceable if its origin as well as its realization and its relation to other documents can be retraced. This can be done by means of unique requirement identifiers. Using these unique identifiers, requirements that are derived from other requirements on a different level of the specification can be connected. For example, a system goal can be traced through all levels of abstraction, from design to implementation and test. Details can be found in section 8.4.

- *Complete*: [ISO/IEC/IEEE 29148:2011] Each individual requirement must completely describe the functionality it specifies. Requirements that are yet incomplete must be specially marked, for example by inserting "tbd" ("to be determined") into the respective text field or by setting a corresponding status. These markings can then be systematically searched for and missing information can be amended accordingly.

- *Understandable*: Requirements must be comprehensible to each stakeholder. Therefore, the type of requirements documentation (see section 4.2) can vary significantly, depending on the development phase (and therefore, depending on the involved staff). In requirements engineering, it is important to strictly define the terms used.

Along with quality criteria for requirements, there are two fundamental rules that enhance the readability of requirements:

Fundamental principles of understandability

- *Short sentences and short paragraphs:* As human short-term memory is very limited, circumstances that belong together should be described in no more than seven sentences.
- *Formulate only one requirement per sentence:* Formulate requirements using active voice and use only one process verb. Long, complicated interlaced sentences must be avoided.

4.7 Glossary

A frequent cause for conflicts in requirements engineering is that the people that are involved in the development process have different interpretations of terms. In order to avoid these conflicts, it is necessary that everyone who is involved in the development process shares the same understanding of the terminology used. Therefore, all relevant terms must be defined in a common glossary. A glossary is a collection of term definitions and contains the following elements:

- Context-specific technical terms
- Abbreviations and acronyms
- Everyday concepts that have a special meaning in the given context
- Synonyms, i.e., different terms with the same meaning
- Homonyms, i.e., identical terms with different meanings

By defining the meaning of terms, you can increase the understandability of requirements considerably. Misunderstandings and different interpretations of terms that might lead to conflicts can be avoided from the beginning.

Consistent definitions

Often, in different projects, terms are used that are similar to one another or in fact identical. This may be the case, for example, when one system is developed for different customers but within the same domain. In this case, already existing glossary entries should be reused. It may even be feasible to define such terms in a universal, inter-project glossary. The additional effort of creating such a glossary will pay off in future projects.

Reuse of glossary entries

For certain domains, collections of term definitions already exist and are publicly accessible. These may serve as the foundation for the definition of specific glossaries. For example, in [IEEE 610.12-1990], typical terms of software engineering are defined.

Rules for Using a Glossary

Basic rules for using a glossary

Since creating a glossary is absolutely mandatory, the following must be noted:

- *The glossary must be centrally managed:* At any time, there must be only one valid glossary, which must also be centrally accessible. There must not be multiple valid glossaries.
- *Responsibility must be assigned:* One particular individual must be assigned with the task of maintaining the glossary and ensuring consistency and up-to-dateness. The necessary resources to accomplish this task must be included in the project plan.
- *The glossary must be maintained over the course of the project:* In order to ensure that the glossary is consistent and up-to-date, it must be maintained over the course of the entire project by the person that was assigned this responsibility.
- *The glossary must be commonly accessible:* The term definitions must be available for all involved personnel. This is the only way a common understanding of the terms can be ensured.
- *Using the glossary must be obligatory:* All involved personnel must be obliged to exclusively use the terms and term definitions as they have been defined in the glossary.
- *The glossary should contain the sources of the terms:* In order to be able to resolve questions and problems at any time during the course of the project, it must be possible to determine the source of a term.
- *The stakeholders should agree upon the glossary:* Only stakeholders can reliably validate the operational definitions for their respective project context. Each definition should be validated by the stakeholders or their representatives. In addition, the individual term definitions in the glossary should be explicitly approved. This approval signals that the respective term is correct and its use is obligatory.
- *The entries in the glossary should have a consistent structure:* All entries in the glossary must be structured in the same way. In order to support a consistent documentation, it is advisable to use a template for glossary definitions. In addition to the definition and the

meaning of a term, the template should specify possible synonyms and homonyms.

To reduce the effort of aligning terms with one another, it is advisable to start with the creation of the glossary early on in the project.

4.8 Summary

The documentation of requirements plays a central role in requirements engineering. As the amount of requirements is often vast, it is very important to clearly structure the requirements so that personnel not involved with the project also understand them. Also, looking up and changing requirements is simplified and accelerated in this way. This makes meeting the quality criteria for requirements documents much easier. Using customized documentation structures has proven to be suitable for that purpose. These are completed by inserting project-specific requirements written in natural language in conjunction with conceptual requirements models.

5 Documenting Requirements in Natural Language

Elicited requirements for the system to be developed are frequently documented using natural language. Natural language has the advantage that it (allegedly) does not require preparation time in order to be read and understood by stakeholders [Robertson and Robertson 2006]. In addition, natural language is universal in the sense that it can be used to describe any circumstances. However, there are some problems associated with the use of natural language for requirements documentation.

5.1 Effects of Natural Language

As natural language is inherently ambiguous and statements in natural language can often be interpreted in multiple ways, it is necessary to place special emphasis on potential ambiguities in such statements to satisfy the criterion of unambiguousness. Requirements are defined and read by people with different knowledge, different social backgrounds, and different experiences. The diversity among the people involved in the development processes may lead to misunderstanding as humans interpret information differently (they form a so-called "deep structure" in their mind) and thus construe it differently as well (e.g., as a requirement). During such a process (i.e., perception and representation of information), so-called "transformational effects" occur that show different characteristics with every human but may occur in all humans [Bandler and Grinder 1975, Bandler 1994].

Subjective perception

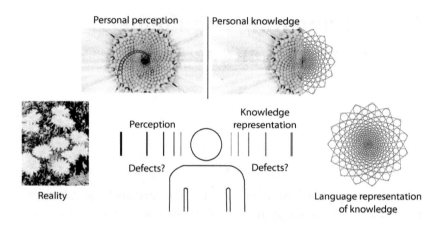

Figure 5-1 *Transformational effects in perception and representation of knowledge*

Transformational effects   The fact that transformational effects adhere to certain rules can be exploited by the requirements engineer to elicit the deep structure (i.e., what the author of a requirement really meant) from its surface structure (i.e., the requirements). The following list includes the five transformational processes that are most relevant for requirements engineering:

- Nominalization
- Nouns without reference index
- Universal quantifiers
- Incompletely specified conditions
- Incompletely specified process verbs

5.1.1   Nominalization

Reduction of processes   By means of nominalization, a (sometimes long-lasting) process is converted into a (singular) event. All information necessary to accurately describe the process is thereby lost. The process word *transmit* turns into the noun *transmission*. Other typical examples of nominalization are the terms *input*, *booking*, and *acceptance*.

Example 5-1: *Nominalization*

"In case of a system crash, a restart of the system shall be performed."
The terms *system crash* and *restart* each describe a process that ought to be analyzed more precisely.

Per se, there are no arguments against the use of nominalized terms to describe complex processes. However, the process should be explicitly defined by the term used. The definition of a nominalized term must not allow for any leeway in the interpretation of the processes and must precisely depict the process, including any exceptions that may occur as well as all input and output parameters. It is therefore not necessary to avoid nominalizations, but they should only be used if the underlying process is completely defined. During the linguistic analysis of a text, all nominalizations ought to be examined to determine whether they have been defined in sufficient detail in another part of the requirements document and whether they are clear for all stakeholders. If this is not the case, another requirement or a glossary entry must be created.

Define processes completely.

5.1.2 Nouns without Reference Index

As with process verbs, nouns are frequently incompletely specified. Linguists call this a missing or inadequate index of reference. Examples of terms that contain incompletely specified nouns are *the user, the controller, the system, the message, the data,* or *the function.*

Nouns with missing reference

Example 5-2: *Nouns without reference indices*

The data shall be displayed to the user on the terminal.

The following questions arise: What data exactly? Which user exactly? Which terminal exactly? If this information is amended, the requirement might thus read as follows:

Example 5-3: *Nouns with added reference indices*

The system shall display the billing data to the registered user on the terminal she is logged in to.

5.1.3 Universal Quantifiers

Universal quantifiers specify amounts or frequencies. They group a set of objects and make a statement about the behavior of this set. When using universal quantifiers, there is the risk that the specified behavior or property does not apply to all objects within the specified set. Stakeholders tend to group objects together, even though some of these objects might

Specify amounts and frequencies.

be special cases or exceptions, where the behavior specified does not apply to all the objects of a group.

Identify universal quantifiers.   It must be verified whether the specified behavior really applies to all objects summarized through the quantifiers. Universal quantifiers can be easily identified through trigger words such as *never, always, no, none, every, all, some,* or *nothing.*

Example 5-4: *Universal quantifiers*

The system shall show all data sets in every submenu.

In this case, the following question must be asked: Really in every submenu? Really all data sets?

5.1.4   Incompletely Specified Conditions

Identify and clarify condition structures. Incompletely specified conditions are another indicator of a potential loss of information. Requirements that contain conditions specify the behavior that must occur when the condition is met. In addition, they must specify what behavior must occur if the condition is not met (the part that is often missing). Especially in complex conditional structures, decision tables can be invaluable tools to find unspecified variants of conditions or actions. Trigger words are, for instance, *if … then, in case, whether,* and *depending on.*

Example 5-5: *Incompletely specified condition*

The restaurant system shall offer all beverages to a registered guest over the age of 20 years.

At least one aspect remains unspecified in the example above: Which beverages shall be offered to a guest that is 20 years or younger? Clarifying this question may lead to extending the requirement as follows:

Example 5-6: *More completely specified condition*

The restaurant system shall offer

All alcohol-free beverages to any registered user younger than 21 years

All beverages including all alcoholic beverages to any user over the age of 20

5.1.5   Incompletely Specified Process Verbs

Some process verbs require more than one noun to be considered com-   *Completing*
pletely specified. The verb *transmit*, for instance, requires at least three   *process words*
supplements to be considered complete: *what* is being transmitted, *from
where* it is being transmitted, and *to where* it is being transmitted. The feel
for language (also referred to as "Sprachgefühl") is a valuable tool to help
gauge which process word must be supplemented in order to be considered
complete. Similarly, adjectives and adverbs may need to be supplemented
as well. While the effect is much less frequent with these types of words
than with verbs, it is often hard to recognize.

The use of incompletely specified process words can mostly be   *Avoid passive voice.*
avoided or kept to a minimum if requirements are formulated using the
active voice rather than the passive voice.

Example 5-7: *Requirement using the passive voice*

To log a user in, the login data is entered.

In this requirement using passive voice, it is unclear who enters the login   *Use active voice.*
data. It is also unclear where and how this is done. If this requirement is
reformulated using the active voice, at least the agent or person responsible
must be included.

The same requirement using active voice might be as follows:

Example 5-8: *Requirement using active voice*

The system must allow the user to enter his user name and password using the
keyboard of the terminal.

5.2   Requirement Construction using Templates

Requirements templates provide a simple and easily understandable   *Quality by means of*
approach to reduce language effects when documenting requirements.   *requirements templates*
Templates support the author in achieving high quality and syntactic   *and glossaries*
unambiguousness in optimal time and at low costs.

Definition 5-1: *Requirements Template*

A requirements template is a blueprint for the syntactic structure of individual
requirements.

In order to achieve lexical clearness in the documentation as well, it is wise to use requirements templates in conjunction with project glossaries (see section 4.7).

The following is a step-by-step description of the correct application of requirements templates.

Step 1: Determine the Legal Obligation

How legally binding is a requirement?

In the beginning, you should determine the degree of legal obligation for a requirement. Usually, one distinguishes between legally obligatory requirements, urgently recommended requirements, future requirements, and desirable requirements. To achieve this within a requirement, you can use the modal verbs *shall*, *should*, *will*, and *may*. Alternatively, the legal obligation of a requirement can be documented by a specific requirements attribute.

Step 2: The Requirement Core

Determine the required process.

The core of each requirement is the functionality that it specifies (e.g., print, save, paste, or calculate). This functionality is referred to as the *process*. Processes are activities and may only be described using verbs. The process that depicts the system behavior by means of a requirement is to be described in step 2.

Since process words determine semantics, they must be defined as clearly as possible and be used as consistently as possible (see section 4.7).

Step 3: Characterize the Activity of a System

For functional requirements, the system activity can be classified as one of three relevant types:

- *Autonomous system activity:* The system performs the process autonomously.
- *User interaction:* The system provides the process as a service for the user.
- *Interface requirement:* The system performs a process depending on a third party (e.g., another system). The system is passive and waits for an external event.

In step 3, any kind of system activity that is specified by a requirement of the system is documented using exactly one of three requirements templates. These requirements templates are described in more detail in the following sections.

After performing steps 1 through 3, the structure of the requirement has been developed (see figure 5-2). The words that are written in angle brackets must be replaced accordingly.

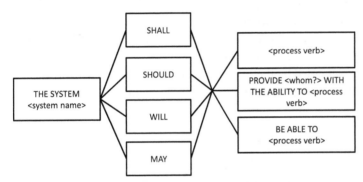

Figure 5-2 *The core of a requirement and its legal obligation*

The first template type is used when requirements are constructed that depict system activities that are performed autonomously. The user does not interact with the activity. We define the following requirements template:

Type 1:
Autonomous system activity

> THE SYSTEM SHALL/SHOULD/WILL/MAY <process verb>

<Process verb> depicts a process verb as described in step 2, e.g., *print* for print functionality or *calculate* for some calculation that is performed by the system.

If the system provides a functionality to a user (for example, by means of an input interface), or the system directly interacts with a user, requirements are constructed using template type 2:

Type 2:
User interaction

> THE SYSTEM SHALL/SHOULD/WILL/MAY provide <whom?> with the ability to <process verb>

The user that interacts with the system is integrated into the requirement through <whom?>.

If the system performs an activity and is dependent on neighboring systems, the third template type is to be used. Whenever messages or data

Type 3:
Interface requirement

are received from a neighboring system, the system must react by executing specific behavior. The following template has proven itself as well suited:

> THE SYSTEM SHALL/SHOULD/WILL/MAY be able to <process verb>

Step 4: Insert Objects

Complete process verbs. Some process verbs require one or more additional objects to be considered complete (see section 5.1.5). In step 4, potentially missing objects and supplements of objects (adverbials) are identified and added to the requirement. For instance, the requirements template for the process verb *print* is amended by the information of *what* is being printed and *where* it is printed. The amendment can be seen in figure 5-3.

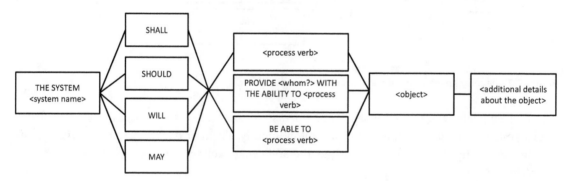

Figure 5-3 *Principle of a complete requirements template without conditions*

Step 5: Determine Logical and Temporal Conditions

Add conditions. Typically, requirements do not document continuous functionalities, but functionalities that are performed or provided only under certain logical or temporal constraints. In order to easily differentiate between logical and temporal conditions, we choose the temporal conjunction *as soon as* for temporal conditions and the conditional conjunction *if* for logical conditions. The conjunction *when* makes not clear whether a temporal or a logical condition is described and should therefore be avoided. In step 5, quality requirements that describe the conditions under which a requirement is fulfilled are added to the beginning of a requirement as a subordinate clause.

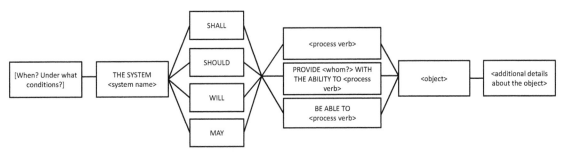

Figure 5-4 *The complete requirements template with conditions*

Requirements templates should be used when project members show interest in a formal development process. Style and creativity are harshly limited when requirements templates are used. Experience shows it is best not to make the use of requirements templates compulsory, but to offer training on the method and treat it as a supplemental tool.

5.3 Summary

System requirements are frequently documented using natural language. Typical advantages that arise from natural language requirements are good readability of requirements, the fact that natural language can be universally applied to document any circumstance, and the fact that no prior knowledge is necessary regarding the notation. On the other hand, there are a number of disadvantages that arise from the fact that natural language requirements are not formalized, e.g., ambiguity. Since project members interpret requirements differently due to differences in their respective knowledge, social background, and experiences, using natural language for requirements documentation often leads to misunderstanding in practice. These disadvantages can be minimized during requirements documentation—for example, by making use of requirements templates and by checking the requirements against linguistic effects.

6 Model-Based Requirements Documentation

During model-based documentation of requirements in requirements engineering, three types of requirements are documented independently and used in conjunction:

- *Goals* describe intentions of stakeholders or groups of stakeholders. Goals can potentially conflict with one another.
- *Use cases* and *scenarios* document exemplary sequences of system usage. Scenarios are grouped together in use cases.
- *System requirements* (generally referred to as requirements) describe detailed functions and qualities that the system to be developed shall implement or possess. In addition, system requirements provide complete and precise information to serve as input for subsequent development steps.

In practice, requirements are often documented using natural language. However, it can be observed that requirements are increasingly often documented using models. Requirement models are used in addition to natural language requirements documentation and partly replace requirements that would have been documented using natural language.

6.1 The Term *Model*

A model is an image that abstracts from reality or that serves as a abstracted representation of reality that is to be created. Modeling may be applied to material or immaterial objects of an existing reality or a reality to be developed. Similarly to [Stachowiak 1973], we define the term *model* as follows:

Models as abstracting images from reality

Definition 6-1: *Model*

A model is an abstract representation of an existing reality or a reality to be created.

6.1.1   Properties of Models

Every model possesses three important properties that are also the prevalent advantages of models:

- *Mapping of reality*: Every model maps certain aspects of the observed reality onto its modeling elements. Model creation can be descriptive and prescriptive in nature. In the case of descriptive model construction, the resulting model documents the existing reality. In the case of prescriptive model construction, the resulting model serves as a prototype for a fictitious reality. Depending on the perspective, models themselves can be both descriptive and prescriptive at the same time. For example, a model is descriptive with regard to the conception of the stakeholder who is constructing it and prescriptive with regard to the system to be developed.
- *Reduction of reality*: Models reduce the mapped reality. It is common to differentiate between selection and compression. During selection, only particular aspects that are part of the universe of discourse of the system are modeled. In contrast, aspects of the subject-matter of the system are summarized during compression.
- *Pragmatic property*: A model is always constructed for a special purpose and within a special context. The purpose of the model may affect the construction and the purpose-driven reduction of reality within the models. Ideally, a model contains only the information necessary for the respective purpose.

Typically, graphical models are used in requirements engineering. Their modeling elements are conceptualizations of material or immaterial objects, or people, in reality.

6.1.2   Modeling Languages

Syntax and semantics   In order to construct conceptual models, specific modeling languages are used. A modeling language is defined by its syntax and semantics:

- Syntax: The syntax of a modeling language defines the modeling elements to be used and specifies the valid combinations thereof.
- Semantics: The semantics defines the meaning of the individual modeling elements and serves therefore as a foundation for the interpretation of the models of the respective modeling language.

Conceptual modeling languages can be classified as formal, informal, and semiformal, depending on the degree of formalization. The degree of formalization of a modeling language depends on the magnitude of formal definitions (e.g., mathematical calculus) that define the syntax and semantics.

Different degrees of formalization

6.1.3   Requirements Models

Conceptual models that document the requirements of a system are called requirements models. The Unified Modeling Language (UML) is frequently used to construct requirements models [OMG 2007]. UML has developed into the quasi-standard for model-based construction of software systems. It consists of a set of partially complementary modeling languages that are particularly used in requirements engineering to model the requirements of a system from different perspectives. Extensive examples of modeling using UML can be found in [Rupp et al. 2007], for instance.

A considerable difference between the conventional use of conceptual models in system development and model usage for requirements documentation is that conventional models document solutions chosen during system development. Requirements models, on the other hand, depict specific aspects of the underlying problem.

Requirements models vs. design models

6.1.4   Advantages of Requirements Models

Research on human cognition has shown that information can be perceived and memorized faster and better when depicted graphically as opposed to making use of natural language. (e.g., [Glass and Holyoak 1986], [Kosslyn 1988], and [Mietzel 1998]. These findings can be applied to the use of requirements models in particular.

Increased understandability

An additional advantage when using requirements models is that in contrast to natural language, the modeling languages used have a strictly defined focus. An example is the different kinds of maps that can be drawn for a city. Depending on what aspect of the city is being mapped (modeled), different types of abstraction can be used to construct the map. For instance, a subway map will show underground subway stations and subway lines. However, the length of each connection on the map may not accurately depict the distance between the stations but may estimate the transit time instead. In contrast to a subway map of a city, a road map of a city accurately depicts the streets, paths, and locations of sights. Both

Support perspectives of documentation.

models depict the same reality, but with a different focus that defines purpose-driven abstractions.

Requirements models also have the advantage that the different types of modeling elements within the same modeling language dictate the method of abstraction as well as what is being abstracted and what is not.

6.1.5   Combined Use of Models and Natural Language

Using both natural language and requirements models in combination allows the advantages of both documentation techniques to be exploited while minimizing their disadvantages. For example, natural language requirements can be summarized and their interrelations depicted using models. On the other hand, natural language can help enrich requirements models and modeling elements with additional information.

6.2   Goal Models

Many methods in requirements engineering are based on the explicit consideration of stakeholders' intentions by means of goals (e.g., [van Lamsweerde et al. 1991] and [Yu 1997]). Ordinarily, the effort required to explicitly consider goals during requirements engineering is minimal. However, the positive impact on requirements engineering—if goals are modeled—and on the quality and comprehensiveness of the requirements is very high. Goals are a stakeholder's (e.g., a person's or an organization's) description of a characteristic property of the system to be developed or the development project.

Natural-language-based and model-based documentation

Goals are very well suited to refine the vision of the system. Refining a goal is known as goal decomposition. Goals can be documented using natural language (e.g., by means of predesigned templates) or using goal models. A widely known and very common goal modeling technique is the use of AND/OR trees. By means of AND/OR trees, hierarchical decompositions can be documented. The type of refinement relation is depicted by graphic representations of the branches. The direction of the goal decomposition is not represented through branches but through the top-down structure of the tree.

6.2.1   Goal Documentation Using AND/OR Trees

Using AND/OR trees, two types of decomposition relationships can be distinguished. Figure 6-1 schematically shows these types of decomposition as well as their modeling elements.

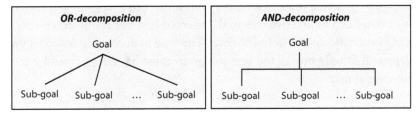

Figure 6-1 *Modeling of goal decomposition using AND/OR trees*

With regard to decomposition relations, one can differentiate between AND-decomposition and OR-decomposition. In case of AND-decomposition, every sub-goal must be fulfilled so that the super-goal (the root) is fulfilled. In contrast, in OR-decomposition, it suffices if at least one sub-goal is fulfilled so that the super-goal is met.

AND-decomposition vs. OR-decomposition

6.2.2   Example of AND/OR Trees

Figure 6-2 shows an AND/OR tree that documents the hierarchical decomposition of the goal "Comfortable navigation to destination".

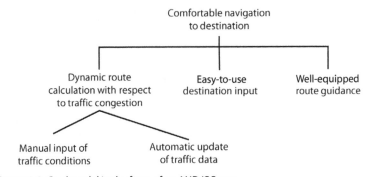

Figure 6-2 *Goal model in the form of an AND/OR tree*

Modeling goals with AND/OR trees

As the goal model in figure 6-2 shows, the goal "comfortable navigation to destination" is refined into the three sub-goals "dynamic route calculation with respect to traffic congestion", "comfortable destination input", and "comfortable route guidance" via AND-decomposition. This depicts that all three sub-goals must be met to consider the super-goal fulfilled. The sub-goal "dynamic route calculation with respect to traffic congestion" in turn is refined by the two sub-goals "manual input of traffic conditions" and "automatic update of traffic data". The type of decomposition relation depicts that only one of the two sub-goals must be met to consider the super-goal met.

6.3   Use Cases

Use cases were first proposed in [Jacobson et al. 1992] as a method to document the functionalities of a planned or existing system on the basis of simple models. The use case approach is based on two concepts that are used in conjunction with one another:

- Use case diagrams
- Use case specifications

6.3.1   UML Use Case Diagrams

Relations between use cases

Use case diagrams in the UML [OMG 2007] (see section 4.2.3) are simple models to schematically document the functions of a system from a user's perspective and to document the interrelations of the functions of a system and the relations between these functions and their environment.

Modeling Elements of UML Use Case Diagrams

Figure 6-3 shows the most essential modeling elements of use case diagrams, as defined in the Unified Modeling Language (UML) [OMG 2007].

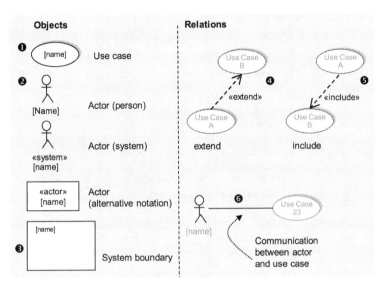

Figure 6-3 *Essential modeling elements of use case diagrams*

❶ *Use cases:* Uses cases that are defined for the system are depicted using oval shapes. These shapes contain the name of the use case. Alternatively, the name can be written beneath the use case.

❷ *Actors:* Actors are outside the system boundary and represent people or systems that interact with the system modeled. Actors are depicted by a rectangle that receives the name of the actor and is tagged with the stereotype "actor". If the actor is a person, a stick figure may be used. If the actor is a system, either a rectangle or a stick figure may be used in conjunction with the stereotype "system".

❸ *System boundaries:* System boundaries within a use case diagram separate the parts of the use case that are part of the system from the parts (people or systems) that are outside the system boundary. Optionally, the name of the system may be denoted at the system boundary in the diagram.

❹ *Extend relation:* An extend relation depicts that an interaction sequence that belongs to use case A extends some interaction sequence in use case B at a specified point. This is known as the extension point. The extension is triggered by the condition defined.

❺ *Include relation:* An include relation from one use case to another use case depicts that the interaction sequence of the first use case includes the interaction sequence of the other use case.

❻ *Relation between actors and use cases:* If communication between a use case and one or more actors takes place during the execution of the use case, the communication must be annotated by means of a communication relation between the respective actors and the use case.

Example of UML Use Case Diagrams

Figure 6-4 shows an example of a use case diagram.

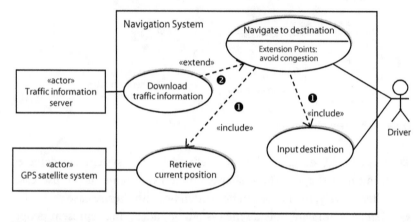

Figure 6-4 *An example using modeling elements of use case diagrams*

The model comprises the use cases "download traffic information", "retrieve current position", and "input navigate to destination" elements. The relations in figure 6-4 that are labeled by numbers are explained in further detail below:

Include ❶ The use case "navigate to destination" is related to the use cases "input destination" and "retrieve current position" via an include relation. The relationship depicts that the interaction steps defined in the use cases "input destination" and "retrieve current position" are contained in the use case "navigate to destination".

Extend ❷ The extend relation between the use cases "download traffic information" and "navigate to destination" defines that the interaction steps defined in the use case "download traffic information" are included in the interaction steps of the use case "navigate to destination" if a certain condition, such as "avoid congestion", is met. The extension point "avoid congestion" depicts the step in the use case "navigate to destination" at which the additional interaction steps are being executed.

UML also provides a generalization relation between use cases or actors. In this case, the specializing use cases or actors inherit the properties of the generalizing use case or actor (e.g., [Rumbaugh et al. 2005]). For instance, the actors "service mechanic" and "customer service representative" can be generalized as the actor "employee". The generalizing actor would carry all aspects that the actors "service mechanic" and "customer service representative" have in common (e.g., employee ID).

Generalization

6.3.2   Use Case Specifications

Use case diagrams show the system's relevant functions from a user's perspective and specific relationships between the functions of the system or between functions of the system and aspects in the system's context. With the exception of a use case's name and its relationships, use cases diagrams do not document any information about the individual use cases such as the systematic interaction between a use case and an actor. This information is documented textually by means of adequate templates in conjunction with use case diagrams.

Pertinent literature proposes different templates for textual specification of use cases (e.g., [Cockburn 2001]). These templates define types of information that should be documented for a use case and suggest an appropriate structure for the information. The template references therefore document experience-based knowledge regarding structured textual documentation of use cases. In order to textually specify use cases, the template in table 6-1 is suitable.

Reference templates for the documentation of use cases

Template for Textual Use Case Documentation		
Nr.	**Section**	**Content / Explanation**
1	Designation	Unique designation of the use case.
2	Name	Unique name of the use case.
3	Authors	Names of the authors that were involved in this use case description.
4	Priority	Importance of the use case according to the applied prioritization technique.
5	Criticality	Criticality of the use case, e.g., with respect to how much damage a failure of the use case may cause.
6	Source	Designation of the source from which the use case was elicited ([stakeholder | document | system]).
7	Person responsible	The stakeholder who is responsible for this use case.
8	Description	Brief description of the use case.
9	Trigger event	Name of the event that triggers this use case.
10	Actors	List of all actors that are involved in this use case.
11	Pre-conditions	List with all necessary constraints that must be met before the use case can begin execution.
12	Post-conditions	List of all states the system can be in immediately after the execution of the main scenario.
13	Result	Description of the results that are produced during use case execution.
14	Main scenario	Description of the main scenario of the use case.
15	Alternative scenarios	Description of the alternative scenarios of the use case or list of the trigger events of alternative scenarios. Often, post-conditions different than those described in (12) may hold.
16	Exception scenarios	Description of the exception scenarios of the use case or list of the trigger events of exception scenarios. Often, post-conditions different than those described in (12) may hold.
17	Qualities	Cross references to quality requirements.

Table 6-1 *Template for textual use case documentation*

Rows of a use case template   The template for the specification of use cases contains the following attributes:

- Attributes for unique identification of use cases (rows 1 and 2)
- Management attributes (rows 3 through 7)
- Attribute for the description of the use case (row 8)
- Specific use case attributes, e.g., the trigger event (row 9), actors (row 10), pre- and post-conditions (rows 11 and 12), the result of the use

case (row 13), the main scenario (row 14), alternative and exception scenarios (rows 15 and 16), and cross references to quality requirements (row 17)

Table 6-2 shows the specification of the use case "navigate to destination" by means of the reference template suggested in table 6-1.

Section	Content
Designation	UC-12-37
Name	Navigate to destination
Authors	John Smith, Sandra Miller
Priority	Importance for system success: **high** Technological risk: **high**
Criticality	High
Source	C. Warner (domain expert for navigation systems)
Responsible	J. Smith
Description	The driver of the vehicle types the name of the destination. The navigation system guides the driver to the desired destination.
Trigger event	The driver wishes to navigate to his destination.
Actors	Driver, traffic information server, GPS satellite system
Pre-condition	The navigation system is activated.
Post-condition	The driver has reached his destination.
Result	Route guidance to the destination
Main scenario	1. The navigation system asks for the desired destination. 2. The driver enters the desired destination. 3. The navigation system pinpoints the destination in its maps. 4. On the basis of the current position and the desired destination, the navigation system calculates a suitable route. 5. The navigation system compiles a list of waypoints. 6. The navigation system shows a map of the current position and shows the route to the next waypoint. 7. When the last waypoint is reached, the navigation system shows "destination reached" on the screen.

Alternative scenario	4a. Calculation of the route must honor traffic information and avoid traffic congestions.
	    4a1. The navigation system queries the server for updated traffic information.
	    4a2. The navigation system calculates a route that does not contain any traffic congestions.

Exception scenarios	Trigger event: The navigation system does not receive a GPS signal from the GPS satellite system.
Qualities	→ QR.04 (reaction time upon user input) → QR.15 (operating comfort) *(QR = quality requirements)*

Table 6-2 *Example of template-based documentation of a use case*

6.4   Three Perspectives on the Requirements

Separately documenting the perspectives

When documenting requirements on the basis of models, one typically distinguishes three types of perspectives: data, function, and behavior (see section 4.2.1). Each perspective is documented separately, using suitable conceptual modeling languages [Davis 1993], [Pohl et al. 2005]:

- *Data perspective:* In this perspective, the structures of input and output data as well as static-structural aspects of the usage and dependency relationships of the system in the system context are documented.
- *Functional perspective:* This perspective documents which information of the system context is being manipulated by the system to be developed and which data is being transmitted to the system context by the system.
- *Behavioral perspective:* The embedding of the system in the system context is documented on the basis of states in this perspective. This is done, for instance, by documenting the reaction of the system to events within the system context, documenting the conditions that trigger a state change, or documenting the effects that the system has on its environment.

Examples of the three perspectives

Figure 6-5 illustrates the three perspectives on functional requirements and gives an example of a suitable modeling language for each perspective that can be used to document the requirements. This way, requirements aspects that pertain to the static structure can be modeled using UML class diagrams, for instance. Requirements in the functional perspective can be modeled using UML activity diagrams and requirements in the behavioral perspective can be modeled using statecharts (see sections 6.6 and 6.7).

Perspectives are not disjoint.

Certain aspects of the models of a particular perspective can also be found in other perspectives. The three perspectives are therefore not disjoint. For example, the data, whose static structure is defined in a UML class diagram can potentially also be found in the functional perspective because it depicts the inputs and outputs of actions in a UML activity diagram. As the three perspectives are not disjoint, the models can be reciprocally checked for completeness and consistency with regard to the information that is modeled at the intersections.

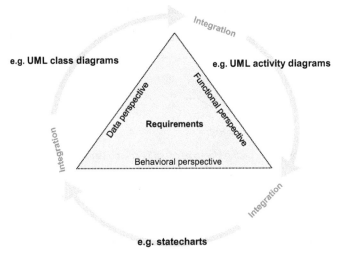

Figure 6-5 *Three perspectives on requirements*

6.5   Requirements Modeling in the Data Perspective

Several different modeling languages are well suited to modeling structural aspects of requirements in the data perspective. Commonly, entity-relationship models, extensions of the traditional entity-relationship model according to Chen [Chen 1976.], and, increasingly, class diagrams of the UML (e.g., [Rumbaugh et al. 2005]) are used as requirements models of the data perspective.

6.5.1   Entity-Relationship Diagrams

Traditionally, entity-relationship diagrams are used for modeling the data perspective because they display the structure of an object of an universe of discourse by means of entity types and relation types [Chen 1976].

The traditional entity-relationship model

A number of extensions for the entity-relationship model have been suggested. These extensions mainly concern the generalization/specialization relations, inheritance mechanisms, and roles of entities and extend the model by a (min, max)-notation for cardinalities of relations.

Extensions of the entity-relationship model

Modeling Elements of Entity-Relationship Diagrams

According to [Chen 1976], the modeling language used to construct entity-relationship diagrams includes the modeling elements depicted in figure 6-6.

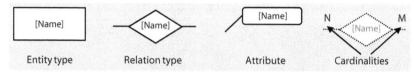

| Entity type | Relation type | Attribute | Cardinalities |

Figure 6-6 *Important modeling elements of entity-relationship diagrams according to Chen*

Classification: abstraction from concrete objects

Entity types define a set of entities within the universe of discourse (that is, objects with the same properties, such as people or items). An entity type (often mistakenly referred to as an entity) abstracts from the concrete characteristics of these entities and therefore classifies a set in the sense of the classification of uniform entities. For instance, the entity type "pilot" classifies all people within the universe of discourse that have the characteristic of holding a piloting license.

Abstraction from concrete relationships

A *relation type* abstracts from a concrete characteristic of a relationship and of entities that are in relation to one another. A relation type classifies the set of uniform relations between entity types within the universe of discourse. For example the relation type "executes" can be defined between the two entity types "pilot" and "flight" to represent concrete "executes"-relations between concrete pilots and concrete flights. If a concrete "is_passenger" relation is defined between a concrete passenger "John Locke"[4] and a concrete flight with the flight number "OA 815"[5], then this relation depicts that "John Locke" is a passenger of the flight with the flight number "OA 815".

Properties of entity types and relation types

An *attribute* can be defined for entity types as well as relation types. An attribute defines the properties of an entity type or a relation type. Possible attributes for the entity type "passenger" could be "family name", "given name", "passport number", and "reserved seat", for instance.

Sketch level vs. instance level

An entity-relationship model documents the structure of a universe of discourse by means of entity types (i.e., classes of uniform entities) and

---

4.   More precisely, there is an entity that is an instance of the entity type "passenger" that possesses a unique identity and has the attribute value "John Locke" for the attribute "name".

5.   More precisely, there is an entity that is an instance of the entity type "flight" that possesses a unique identity and has the attribute value "OA 815" for the attribute "flight number".

relations (i.e., classes of uniform relationships). An entity-relationship model is defined on the modeling level and defines the set of all valid instances on the instance level.

The *cardinality* of a (binary) relation defines the number of relation instances that an entity may participate in [Elmasri and Navathe 2006]. If no cardinalities are annotated for a specific relation type, it is assumed that an arbitrary number of entities (in other words, at least zero entities) may participate in such a relation. Using cardinalities for relations therefore limits the number of instances that are principally possible in an entity-relationship diagram.

Number of relation instances

Example of an Entity-Relationship Diagram

The entity-relationship model shown in figure 6-7 shows four entity types (i.e., classes of entities) and three relation types (i.e., classes of relationships). The individual entity types possess attributes that describe specific properties of the associated entities. For example, the entity type "traffic jam information" has the attributes "road", "start", and "length", which depict the road on which a traffic jam is currently present, the GPS coordinates of the starting point of the jam, and the length of the jam. The relation type "queries" between the entity types "navigation device" and "traffic jam information" means that on the instance level, a relationship between a concrete navigation device and the information on zero or more concrete traffic jams exists. The cardinalities of the entity types with regard to the relation type "queries" means that a concrete navigation device can query information on an arbitrary amount ("N") of traffic jams. In the other direction, any traffic jam information can be queried by an arbitrary number ("M") of navigation devices.

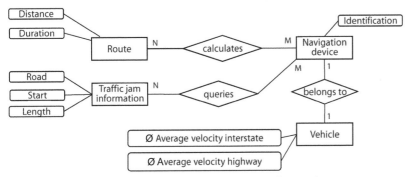

***Figure 6-7** Entity-relationship diagram (data model) according to Chen*

6.5.2   UML Class Diagrams

Static perspective: data/
structure
Class diagrams of the UML can be used to model the data perspective of requirements of a system to be developed as well. A class diagram consists of a set of classes and associations between classes. Classes and associations in UML class diagrams are similar to entity types and relation types in entity-relationship diagrams. Class models possess additional modeling elements (e.g., that allow for the specification of valid operations on the instances of a class) and thus have a greater power of description.[6]

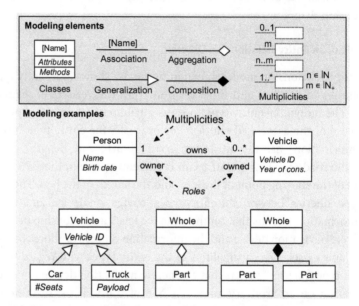

Figure 6-8 *Important modeling elements of class diagrams of UML*

Modeling Elements of Class Diagrams

Figure 6-8 shows important modeling elements of class diagrams of the UML as well as a number of modeling examples.

Classes
A *class* is depicted by a rectangle that is separated into sections (also called *compartments*). In the upper section, attributes are depicted that are described in more detail by the instances of the class. In the lower sections, all operations that can be performed on the instances of the class are listed. Depending on the modeling goal, i.e., depending on the purpose of the

---

6.   A comprehensive overview of the different modelling elements of the UML can be found e.g., in [OMG 2007].

model, the compartments for attributes and/or methods can also be hidden or left out entirely.

Associations between classes are depicted by edges. Associations can optionally be given a name. In addition, *multiplicities* can be annotated at each end of an association. Multiplicities are statements about the instance level of a class and depict how many instances of a class may be associated in a particular way with a defined number of instances of another class. By annotating optional *roles* at one or both ends of an association, the meaning of the instances of a class with regard to the association can the further refined.

Associations, multiplicities, and roles

Aggregations and *compositions* are specific types of associations. Both describe a relationship between a whole and its constituents. A composition documents a stronger binding than an aggregation in that a constituent in a composition cannot exist without its whole. In class models of the UML, an aggregation is depicted as an empty diamond and a composition is depicted as a filled diamond.

Aggregation and composition

Moreover, in class diagrams, *generalizations* between classes can be documented. A generalization between classes of the UML is a relationship between a more specific class (the sub-type) and a more general class (the super-type). The sub-type in a generalization relation inherits all properties of the super-type and can adapt and/or extend these.

Generalization

Example of a UML Class Diagram

The class diagram in figure 6-9 comprises six classes that all have respective attributes. The associations between the classes are depicted by means of edges. For example, an association with the name "calculates" exists between the class "navigation device" and the class "route". Taking into account the multiplicities, this association depicts that a navigation system can calculate an arbitrary amount (at least zero, as depicted by an asterisk *) of routes. In return, every route can be calculated by an arbitrary amount (*) of navigation devices. A route is an aggregation of at least one, but arbitrarily many (1..*) road segments, and every road segment belongs to an arbitrary amount (*) of routes. A road segment is defined by a road name as well as start and end points. Figure 6-9 also shows that "navigation device w/ congestion avoiding" is a specialization of the generic type "navigation device". The sub-type "navigation device w/ congestion avoiding" inherits the properties (in this case, the attribute "identification") from its super-type "navigation device" and extends the set of attributes by an attribute that specifies the threshold length of a traffic congestion, which triggers a route recalculation.

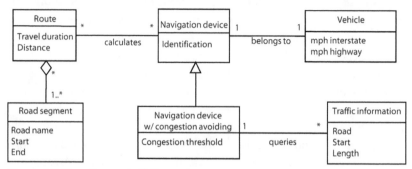

Figure 6-9 *Class diagram in UML notation*

6.6   Requirements Modeling in the Functional Perspective

The functional perspective of requirements deals with the transformation of input data received from the environment into output data released into the environment of the system. There are a number of different model-based approaches that can be used to model the functional perspective of requirements. The majority of these techniques is based on the structured system analysis approaches of the 1970s and 1980s, such as the structured analysis [DeMarco 1978, Weinberg 1978] or the essential system analysis [McMenamin and Palmer 1988.].

6.6.1   Data Flow Diagrams

At the center of attention of modeling requirements from a functional perspective are diagrams that model the functionality of the respective system by means of processes (functions), data stores, sources, and sinks in the system environment as well as data flow. A commonly used type of functional models are data flow diagrams, as suggested in the structured analysis according to [DeMarco 1978]. Data flow models allow modeling the system on different levels of abstraction.

Modeling Elements of Data Flow Diagrams

Figure 6-10 shows the modeling elements in data flow diagrams in the notation suggested by [DeMarco 1978].

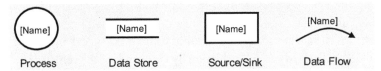

Figure 6-10 *Important modeling elements of data flow diagrams according to DeMarco*

Processes depict the functions of a particular system necessary to transform the data that flows into the system (information flow).[7] A process consumes the input data, processes this data, and outputs the result of the processing in the form of output data. *How* the data is transformed is not depicted in data flow diagrams.

Data manipulation

Data stores are abstract concepts designed to depict persistent data. Processes can access data in a data store in a read and write manner so that the processes may access necessary input data or persistently store output data.

Resting data

Sources/sinks describe objects (like people, groups of people, departments, organizations, or systems) in the environment of the system that exchange data with the system. Sources/sinks are aspects of the system environment and cannot be altered during system development (see section 2.1). Sources are aspects of the system environment that deliver data to the system, while sinks receive data from the system.

Objects in the system environment

A *data flow* describes data that is transported between processes, data stores, and sources/sinks [Yourdon 1989]. In requirements models, a data flow can model both the transport of material and immaterial objects, e.g., information flow or material flow. Typically, only the most important data flows are modeled in data flow diagrams. Data flows that are not relevant for the requirements of the system can be neglected.

Flowing data

Example of a Data Flow Diagram

Figure 6-11 shows a simplified data flow diagram of a navigation system in the notation suggested by DeMarco. The interfaces of the system to the

System interfaces

---

7.   In the structured analysis, the flow of data, information, documents, or material is considered a data flow.

Process "calculate route"

context are defined by the data flows to the sources "GPS satellite system" and "traffic information server" as well as to the sink "driver".

The functionality of the navigation system is separated into three distinct processes. Process one, named "calculate route", receives up-to-date traffic information via its interface to the source "traffic information server" as well as data about the current location via its interface to the source "GPS satellite system". In addition, the process "calculate route" is provided with the desired destination by the driver of the vehicle. The calculated route is stored in the data store "route data".

Process "determine next waypoint"

Process two—"determine next waypoint"—accesses the data store and retrieves data concerning the current route. The process determines the next waypoint and outputs this information.

Process "recalculate route"

Process three—"recalculate route"—plots a new course to the destination. In order to do so, it gathers traffic information from the source "traffic information server" and, potentially, information about the current location. The newly calculated course is stored in the data store "route data".

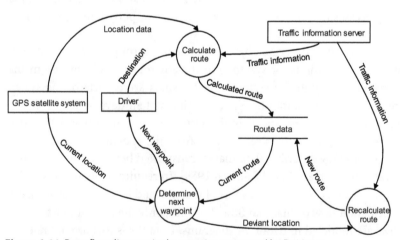

Figure 6-11 *Data flow diagram in the notation suggested by DeMarco*

6.6.2   Models of the Functional Perspective and Control Flow

In data flow diagrams, it cannot be seen which conditions trigger which processes. Data flow diagrams merely depict data dependencies of the processes in a system and document necessary input and generated output data. Approaches used in structured system analysis, however, often offer complementary behavioral descriptions and control flow descriptions.

This is achieved either by using distinct documentation forms, such as mini-specifications in structured analysis, or by means of implicit language extensions of data flow models. Language extensions offer the ability to model additional aspects, e.g., the control flow between functions, as done in SA/RT [Ward and Mellor 1985, Hatley and Pirbhai 1988].

6.6.3   UML Activity Diagrams

UML activity diagrams are well suited to model action sequences [OMG 2007]. Along with activity diagrams in UML, event-driven process chains (EPC) can be used to model sequences of activities [Keller et al. 1992], especially in information system development. UML activity diagrams depict the control flow between activities or actions. In case of a sequential progression of actions, a subsequent action is executed once every precedent action terminates. Figure 6-12 shows important modeling elements of activity diagrams in UML [OMG 2007].

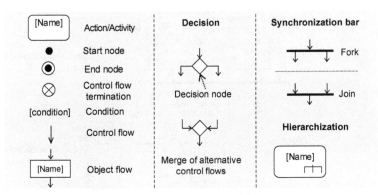

Figure 6-12 *Modeling elements of activity diagrams of the UML*

Activity diagrams are control flow graphs that consist of action nodes and the control flow between these action nodes (i.e., the arrows in the control flow graph depicting transitions). Action nodes execute an action. The start and end nodes in activity diagrams have defined semantics. The start node represents an event that initiates the execution of the activity diagram. End nodes are special nodes that represent the termination of the activity diagram.

Action nodes

Depicting alternative control flows in activity diagrams can be achieved through the use of decision nodes. At decision nodes, conditions that trigger alternative control flows are annotated. In addition, synchro-

Control flows, object flows, responsibilities

nization bars allow for concurrent execution of control flows. A special type of control flows are object flows. By making use of activity partitions (swimlanes), different activities can be documented as the responsibility of specific actors.

Sequence Modeling using UML Activity Diagrams

The activity diagram in figure 6-13 documents the process "navigate to destination". Input and output data can be documented by modeling additional object flows along the edges. The data and object flows are special types of control flows of the activity diagram. Every action is executed if and only if previous actions have been carried out and all incoming object flows are available. The action diagram in figure 6-13 also shows object flows that are documented in addition to the actions and control flows.

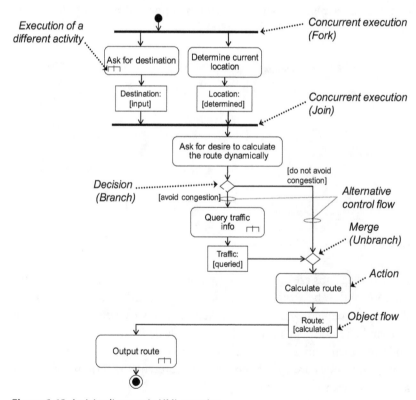

Figure 6-13 *Activity diagram in UML notation*

The activity diagram above documents the sequence of actions necessary for a navigation device to calculate a route. The model documents that initially the desired destination is asked for and that the current location is determined. These two actions happen concurrently, independent from one another. The input destination (object flow: object → destination; state → input) and the determined location (object flow: object → location; state → determined) are relayed. If the driver has opted to automatically circumvent traffic congestions, the system queries for up-to-date traffic information. Once the updated traffic information is received or if the driver has not selected to circumvent traffic jams, the system calculates a route to the destination. The calculated route is output to the driver.

Activity diagrams are well suited to document the relationships and execution conditions of main, alternative, and exception scenarios. Decision nodes represent branches in the control flow between the main scenario and alternative and exception scenarios.

Modeling sequences of a use case

Control Flow of Main and Alternative Scenarios

The activity diagram in figure 6-14 shows the control flow of the main and alternative scenario of the use case "navigate to destination" as documented in table 6-2. Alternative control flow branches begin at the decision nodes that document the respective alternative- and exception scenarios to a particular main scenario.

The activity diagram shows that initially, the action "start navigation" is executed. After that, the actions "input destination" and "determine GPS coordinates" are executed concurrently and independent from one another. Once both actions have been executed, the system asks the driver if he wishes the route to be calculated dynamically (action "ask for desire to calculate the route dynamically"). If the driver does not request the route to be calculated dynamically (selection "do not avoid congestions"), no specific action is executed (see table 6-1 → main scenario). If the driver selects dynamic route calculation (selection "avoid congestions"), updated traffic information is determined (action "query traffic info", see table 6-1 → alternative scenario). After that, the route is calculated (action "calculate route") and output to the driver (action "output route").

Main and alternative scenarios

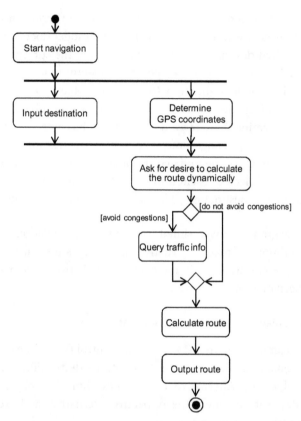

Figure 6-14 *Documentation of the control flow of scenarios using UML activity diagrams*

6.7   Requirements Modeling in the Behavioral Perspective

Finite-state automata

To model the dynamic behavior of a system, modeling approaches based on automata theory are typically employed. The definition of a finite-state automaton comprises a set of states and a set of transitions that, dependent on the current state of the automaton, are performed given some event.

Mealy and Moore automata

In the scope of system modeling, extensions of finite-state automata are frequently used that are based on the concepts of so-called Mealy [Mealy 1955] and Moore automata [Moore 1956], respectively. In Mealy automata, the output of an automaton depends on the current state of the automaton as well as on the input. In contrast, in Moore automata, the output merely depends on the current state.

6.7.1   Statecharts

Due to challenges that arise when using finite state automata in practice (such as missing support for abstraction), the automata concept has been developed into a technique of modeling the reactive behavior of a system. A widely applied technique to model the behavior of a system is the use of statecharts [Harel 1987]. Statecharts are a type of automata that is based on finite-state automata but are extended to support hierarchization of states to document conditions of state transitions and to model concurrent behavior. Figure 6-15 shows the modeling elements of statecharts in the notation suggested by Harel [Harel 1987].

Statecharts =
state machines
+ hierarchization
+ conditions
+ concurrency

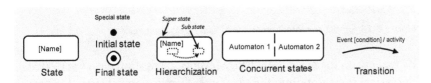

Figure 6-15 *Modeling elements of statecharts*

A state defines a period of time in which the system shows a specific behavior and waits for a particular event to occur in order to perform a defined transition.

State

A transition is triggered by a particular event once it occurs in a specific state. A transition describes the change from one state to the next. The change of states can additionally be dependent on some condition. The system can perform particular activities if it is in a particular state (typical for Moore automata) or if it performs a transition to another state (typical for Mealy automata). These activities can be directed toward the system itself or the environment of the system.

Transition with condition
and activity

Statecharts allow for the hierarchical refinement of states that in turn represent automata. The initial state is referred to as super state and is defined by a number of refining states. Hierarchization allows abstracting from the irrelevant details of a state by—depending on the purpose of the model—only regarding and/or modeling the super state rather than the entire sub automaton that defines the super state. The detailed behavior of the system can, if necessary, be refined by defining the respective partial automata.

Hierarchization and
abstraction

Along with hierarchical decomposition of a state into refining automata, a state can be decomposed into several concurrent automata. The concurrent automata can be synchronized by means of transition conditions

Concurrency

(e.g., "if automaton A is in state 4"). Figure 6-16 shows a behavior model for a navigation device of a vehicle by means of a statechart. The navigation device is initially in the state "navigation device inactive".

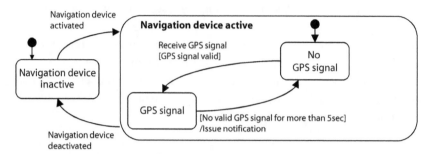

Figure 6-16 *Simplified statechart of a vehicular navigation device*

Transition into super state   By turning on the navigation device (event: "navigation device activated"), the system transitions into the super state "navigation device active" (more precisely, the system transitions into the initial state "no GPS signal" of the super state "navigation device active"). The super state "navigation device active" is refined by a partial automaton that consists of two states. For example, if a GPS signal is received in the state "navigation device active: no GPS signal"[8]. the system transitions into the state "navigation device active: GPS signal" and issues a notification. If the device is deactivated while in the state "navigation device active" (event: "navigation device deactivated"), the system transitions into the state "navigation device inactive".

6.7.2   UML State Diagrams

Modeling reactive behavior   In order to model reactive system behavior, Unified Modeling Language
of a system using UML   (UML) [OMG 2007] offers so-called state machines that are essentially based on statecharts. Figure 6-17 shows the most important modeling elements of UML state diagrams. The notation of the modeling elements of UML state diagrams has largely been adopted from statecharts. However, UML 2 extends the modeling elements of statecharts, e.g., by the ability to define explicit entry and exit points of hierarchical states [OMG 2007].

---

8.   For unique identification, a state that is part of a super state is referenced by "super state: state". The state "no GPS signal" in the super state "navigation device active" is therefore referenced as "navigation device active: no GPS signal".

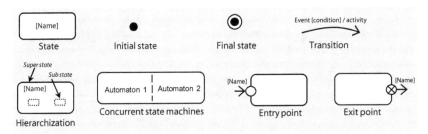

Figure 6-17 *Modeling elements of state machines as defined by the UML 2*

Just as in statecharts, a state defines a period of time in which a system shows a particular behavior and waits for a particular event to occur. A transition is triggered by an event that occurs in a particular state and describes the change from one state to the next. A transition can be dependent on a condition. In addition, the system can perform actions that are directed toward the system or its environment.

States and transitions

Depending on the purpose of the model, state machines allow hierarchically combining states into super states, thereby abstracting from the potentially very complex behavior of these states. Aside from hierarchically decomposing states by means of partial automata, a state can be decomposed into several concurrent state machines. Just as in statecharts, synchronization of concurrent state machines can be achieved using conditions.

Hierarchization and concurrency

UML 2 defines entry points and exit points as an extension of statecharts that allow for additional hierarchization of states. An exit point is an externally visible pseudo-state that is immediately associated with an internal state. An exit point is an externally visible pseudo-state that has its origin in an internal state. A super state within a state machine can have arbitrarily many entry and exit points that can be identified by a name [Rumbaugh et al. 2005].

Encapsulation of internal states using entry and exit points

Figure 6-18 shows a state diagram of UML that possesses two explicitly defined entry points ("enter new destination" and "last destination") as well as one exit point ("navigation successful") along with the modeling elements introduced in section 6.7.1.

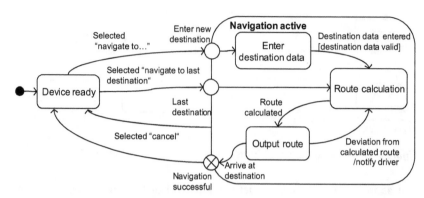

Figure 6-18 *State diagram in UML 2 notation*

The state diagram in figure 6-18 documents the reactive behavior of a navigation device. Initially, the system is in the state "device ready". By selecting "navigate to…", the system changes into the super state "navigation active" and, within the super state, into the sub state "enter destination data" by making use of the entry point "enter new destination". Alternatively, the system changes from the state "device ready" into the internal state "route calculation" of the super state "navigation active" by making use of the entry point "last destination" as soon as the event "navigate to last destination" occurs. Once the system is in the state "navigation active: enter destination data", the system transitions into the state "navigation active: route calculation" if the condition that the destination data is valid has been met.

Once the route is calculated in the state "navigation active: route calculation", the system transitions into the state "navigation active: output route". If a deviation from the route is detected (event: "deviation from calculated route") in the state "navigation active: route calculation", the driver is notified (activity: "notify driver"). From the state "navigation active", the system transitions into the state "device ready" once the event "cancel" occurs. If the system is in the state "navigation active: route calculation" and the destination is reached, the system exits the super state "navigation active" via the exit point "navigation successful" to transition into the state "device ready".

6.8 Summary

Along with using natural language to document requirements, requirements can be documented by means of models. Typically, natural language requirements and requirements models are frequently employed in conjunction so that the advantages of both forms of documentation can be exploited.

Model-based documentation of requirements has, among other things, the advantage that graphical (imagelike) descriptions of circumstances can be understood faster and better than natural-language descriptions. Among the models that are frequently used in requirements engineering are goal models (e.g., in the form of AND/OR trees) and use case diagrams as well as conceptual models to document requirements from three perspectives: data, functional, and behavioral. For each of these three perspectives, there are suitable conceptual modeling languages that provide purpose-specific means to document the information depicted in each respective perspective.

7   Requirements Validation and Negotiation

Validation and negotiation during requirements engineering is meant to ensure that the documented requirements meet the predetermined quality criteria, such as correctness and agreement (see section 4.6). The introduced principles and techniques can be used to validate and negotiate individual requirements or entire requirements documents.

7.1   Fundamentals of Requirements Validation

During the requirements engineering activity, it is necessary to review the quality of the requirements developed. Among others, the requirements are presented to the stakeholders with the goal to identify deviations between the requirements defined and the stakeholders' actual wishes and needs.

During requirements validation, the decision of whether a requirement possesses the necessary level of quality is made (see chapter 4) and whether the requirement can be approved to be used for further development activities (such as design, implementation, and testing). This decision should be made on the basis of predefined acceptance criteria.

Approving requirements

The goal of requirements validation is therefore to discover errors in the documented requirements. Typical examples of errors in requirements are ambiguity, incompleteness, and contradictions (see section 7.3).

Goal of validation

Requirements documents are reference documents for all further development activities. Therefore, errors negatively affect all further development activities. A requirements error that is discovered when the system is already deployed and operating requires all artifacts affected by the error to be revised, such as source code, test artifacts, and architectural descriptions. Correcting errors in requirements once the system is in operation therefore entails significant costs.

Error proliferation

Legal risks   A contract between client and contractor is often based on requirements documents. Critical errors in requirements can lead to the fact that contractual agreements cannot be met, e.g., scope of supply and services, expected quality, or completion deadlines.

7.2 Fundamentals of Requirements Negotiation

Contradictory requirements cause conflicts.   If there is no consent among the stakeholders regarding the requirements and thus the requirements cannot be implemented collectively in the system, a conflict arises between the contradictory requirements as well as between the stakeholders that demand contradictory requirements. For example, one stakeholder could demand the system to shut down in case of a failure, whereas another stakeholder could require the system to restart.

Risks and opportunities of conflicts   The acceptance of a system is threatened by unresolved conflicts because unresolved conflicts cause the requirements of at least one group of stakeholders to not be implemented. In the worst case, a conflict causes stakeholder support to cease, causing the development project to fail (cf. [Easterbrook 1994]). Other than posing risks, conflicts can also be an opportunity for requirements engineering because conflicts between stakeholders require a solution that can potentially help discover new ideas for development and can illustrate different options (cf. [Gause and Weinberg 1989]). Therefore, treating and resolving conflicts openly during requirements engineering can increase acceptance.

Goal of requirements negotiation   The goal of negotiation is to gain a common and agreed-upon understanding of the requirements of the system to be developed among all relevant stakeholders.

Reducing costs and risks in late phases   Requirements validation and negotiation is an activity that must be performed (to a varying degree of intensity) throughout the entirety of requirements engineering. The validation and negotiation of requirements therefore causes additional effort and therefore additional costs. However, the advantages gained by performing requirements validation and negotiation as described in the previous sections (reduction of overall cost, increase in acceptance, supporting creativity and innovations) is usually significantly higher than the costs that arise due to the increased effort.

7.3 Quality Aspects of Requirements

A major aim of using quality criteria (e.g., completeness, understandability, agreement) in requirements validation is to be able to check requirements systematically (see section 1.1.2). In order to assure an objective and consistent validation, it is necessary that each quality criterion is concretized and refined. In correspondence with the overall goals of the requirements engineering process, the validation is carried out with the following goals:

- *Content:* Have all relevant requirements been elicited and documented with the appropriate level of detail?
- *Documentation:* Are all requirements documented with respect to the predetermined guidelines for documentation and specification?
- *Agreement:* Do all stakeholders concur with the documented requirements and have all known conflicts been resolved?

Each of the three goals implies an individual approach that focuses on specific aspects of the quality of the requirements. Therefore, the following three quality aspects have been defined:

Three quality aspects

- Quality aspect "content"
- Quality aspect "documentation"
- Quality aspect "agreement"

A requirement should be approved for further development activities only if all three quality aspects have been checked. The quality aspects are described in detail in the following sections and made concrete through different fine-grained quality criteria (with no claim of completeness).

7.3.1 Quality Aspect "Content"

The quality aspect "content" refers to the validation of requirements with respect to errors in the content. Errors in requirements with regard to content negatively influence the subsequent development activities and cause these activities to be based upon erroneous information.

Errors in requirements with regard to content are present when specific quality criteria for requirements (see section 4.6) or for requirements documents (see section 4.5) are violated. The validation of requirements with regard to the quality aspect "content" is successful once requirements

Test criteria of the quality aspect "content"

validation has been applied to the following error types and no significant shortcomings have been detected:

- *Completeness (set of all requirements):* Have all relevant requirements for the system to be developed (for the next system release) been documented?
- *Completeness (individual requirements):* Does each requirement contain all necessary information?
- *Traceability:* Have all relevant traceability relations been defined (e.g., to relevant requirements sources)?
- *Correctness/adequacy:* Do the requirements accurately reflect the wishes and needs of the stakeholders?
- *Consistency:* Is it possible to implement all defined requirements for the system to be developed jointly? Are there no contradictions?
- *No premature design decisions:* Are there any forestalled design decisions present in the requirements not induced by constraints (e.g., constraints that specifiy a specific client-server architecture to be used)?
- *Verifiability:* Is it possible to define acceptance and test criteria based on the requirements? Have the criteria been defined?
- *Necessity:* Does every requirement contribute to the fulfillment of the goals defined?

7.3.2   Quality Aspect "Documentation"

The quality aspect "documentation" deals with checking requirements with respect to flaws in their documentation or violations of the documentation guidelines that are in effect, such as understandability of the documentation formats and the consideration of organizational or project-specific guidelines regarding the documentation of requirements but also the structure of the requirements documents.

Implications of the violation of documentation guidelines

Ignoring the documentation guidelines can, among other things, lead to the following risks:

- *Impairment of development activities:* It may be impossible to carry out development activities that are based upon a specific documentation format.
- *Misunderstandings:* Requirements may not be understandable or may be misunderstood by the people that need to comprehend them. As a result, the requirement may be unusable.

- *Incompleteness:* Relevant information is not documented in the requirements.
- *Overlooking requirements:* If requirements are not documented at the position that they are supposed to in the requirements document, these requirements may be overlooked in subsequent activities.

Requirements validation with regard to the quality aspect "documentation" is successful when requirements validation has been applied to the following error types and no significant shortcomings have been detected:

Test criteria of the quality aspect "documentation"

- *Conformity to documentation format and to documentation structures:* Are the requirements documented in the predetermined documentation format? For instance, has a specific requirements template or a specific modeling language been used to document the requirements? Has the structure of the requirements document been maintained? For instance, have all requirements been documented at the position defined by the document structure?
- *Understandability:* Can all documented requirements be understood in the context given? For instance, have all terms used been defined in a glossary (see section 4.7)?
- *Unambiguity:* Does the documentation of the requirements allow for only one interpretation or are multiple different interpretations possible? For instance, does a text-based requirement not possess any kind of ambiguity?
- *Conformity to documentation rules:* Have the predetermined documentation rules and documentation guidelines been met? For instance, has the syntax of the modeling language been used properly?

Four test criteria of the quality aspect "documentation"

7.3.3   Quality Aspect "Agreement"

The quality aspect "agreement" deals with checking requirements for flaws in the agreement of requirements between stakeholders.

During the course of requirements engineering, stakeholders gain novel knowledge about the system to be developed. Due to this additional knowledge, the opinion of the stakeholders regarding a requirement that has already been agreed upon can change. During requirements validation, stakeholders have the opportunity to requests changes without impairing the subsequent development activities.

Last opportunity for changes

Requirements validation with regard to the quality aspect "agreement" is successful when requirements validation has been applied to the following error types and no significant shortcomings have been detected:

Three test criteria of the quality aspect "agreement"

▦ *Agreed:* Is every requirement agreed upon with all relevant stakeholders?

▦ *Agreed after changes:* Is every requirement agreed upon with all relevant stakeholders after it has been changed?

▦ *Conflicts resolved:* Have all known conflicts with regard to the requirements been resolved?

7.4   Principles of Requirements Validation

Considering the following six principles of requirements validation increases the quality of the validation results:

▦ *Principle 1:* Involvement of the correct stakeholders
▦ *Principle 2:* Separating the identification and the correction of errors
▦ *Principle 3:* Validation from different views
▦ *Principle 4:* Adequate change of documentation type
▦ *Principle 5:* Construction of development artifacts
▦ *Principle 6:* Repeated validation

The individual principles are explained in the following sections.

7.4.1   Principle 1: Involvement of the Correct Stakeholders

The choice of stakeholders for requirements validation depends on the goals of the validation as well as the requirements that are to be audited.

When assembling the auditing team, at least the following two aspects ought to be considered.

Independence of the auditor

Generally, it should be avoided that the author of a requirement is also the person to validate it. The author will make use of his or her prior knowledge when reading or reviewing the requirement. This prior knowledge can negatively influence the identification of errors because potential erroneous passages of the requirements documentation or the requirements are implicitly and subconsciously amended by the author's own knowledge and can thus easily be overlooked.

Suitable auditors can be identified within or outside of the developing organization. Internal audits are performed by stakeholders that are members of the developing organization and can be used to validate intermediate results or preliminary requirements. An internal validation is easy to coordinate and organize because the stakeholders are available from within the organization. An external audit requires a higher degree of effort because it identifies auditors and (potentially) hires them for payment. In addition, external auditors have to become familiar with the context of the system to be developed. Due to the high effort, an external audit should be performed only on requirements that exhibit a high level of quality.

Internal vs. external auditors

7.4.2   Principle 2: Separating the Identification and the Correction of Errors

Separation between identifying errors and actually fixing them has proven itself in the domain of software quality assurance. The same principle can be applied to requirements validation. During validation, the flaws identified are documented immediately. After that, each flaw identified is double-checked to determine whether it really is an error.

Basic principle

Separating error identification and error correction allows auditors to concentrate on the identification. Measures to correct the errors are taken only after identification measures have been completed. This has the advantages that the resources available for error correction can be used purposefully, that premature error identification does not create additional errors, and that no alleged error is fixed that did not need fixing because further investigation of the error may result in the fact that an alleged error is in fact no error at all. That way, potentially present significant errors are less likely to be overlooked because the auditor is concentrating on fixing a previous error instead of identifying new ones.

Concentrating on error identification

7.4.3   Principle 3: Validation from Different Views

Validating requirements from different views is another principle that has proven itself in practice. In this principle, requirements are validated and agreed upon from different perspectives (e.g., by different people, see section 7.5.4). Comparable methods are used in other disciplines as well. For instance, in a legal trial, circumstances are often reported from the perspective of different people so that a sound overall picture can be gained.

Perspective-based validation

7.4.4   Principle 4: Adequate Change of Documentation Type

Strengths and weaknesses of documentation types

Changing the documentation type during requirements validation uses the strengths of one documentation type to balance out the weaknesses of other documentation types. For instance, good understandability and expressiveness are strengths of natural language texts. However, their weakness is potential ambiguity and difficulty in expressing complex circumstances. Graphic models are able to depict complex circumstances rather well, but the individual modeling constructs are restricted in expressiveness.

Simpler identification of errors

Transcribing a requirement that is already documented in another form of documentation simplifies finding errors. For instance, ambiguities in natural language requirements can be identified much easier by transcribing them into a model-based representation.

7.4.5   Principle 5: Construction of Development Artifacts

Suitability of the requirements for design, test, and manual creation

Constructing development artifacts aims at validating the quality of requirements that are meant to be the basis of creating design artifacts, test artifacts, or the user manual. During the course of the validation, the activities usually carried out during subsequent phases to construct respective development artifacts are carried out for small samples. For instance, the auditor intensively deals with a requirement by creating a test case. This way, errors (e.g., ambiguity) can be identified in the requirement. This kind of validation, however, demands a lot of resources because subsequent development activities must be executed at least in part.

7.4.6   Principle 6: Repeated Validation

Validation occurs at a distinct point in time during the development process and relies on the level of knowledge of the auditors at that point in time. During requirements engineering, the stakeholders gain additional knowledge about the planned system. Therefore, a positive validation of requirements does not guarantee that requirements are still valid at a later point in time. Requirements validation should occur multiple times in the following cases (among others):

- Lots of innovative ideas and technology used in the system
- Significant gain of knowledge during requirements engineering
- Long-lasting projects

- Very early requirements validation
- Unknown domain
- Requirements that are to be reused

7.5   Requirements Validation Techniques

In the following sections, techniques for requirements validation are introduced. Often, manual validation techniques, which are also known by the general term *review*, are used for requirements validation. Three major types of reviews can be differentiated:

- Commenting
- Inspections
- Walk-throughs

Along with reviews, the following three techniques have proven themselves to be useful for requirements validation:

- Perspective-based reading
- Validation through prototypes
- Using checklists for validation

In the following, these six techniques are described. Prior to applying any of these techniques, preparatory steps need to be taken as needed, such as identifying and inviting the right stakeholders or organizing suitable rooms and supplies.

7.5.1   Commenting

During commenting, the author hands his or her requirements over to another person (e.g., a co-worker). The goal is to receive the co-worker's expert opinion with regard to the quality of a requirement. The co-worker reviews the requirement with the goal to identify issues that impair requirement quality (e.g., ambiguity or errors) with respect to predetermined quality criteria. The identified flaws are marked in the requirements document and briefly explained.

Individual validation of requirements

7.5.2   Inspection

Typical phases of an inspection

Inspections of software or any other type of product are done to systematically check development artifacts for errors by applying a strict process [Laitenberger and DeBaud 2000].

An inspection is typically separated into various phases [Gilb and Graham 1993]: planning, overview, defect detection, defect correction, follow-up, and reflection. For requirements validation, the planning, overview, error detection, and error collection phases are relevant (see principle 2, separating the identification and correction of errors in section 7.4.2). Individual preparation is an obligatory part of inspections. An inspection session usually serves the purpose of collecting and evaluating error indications. Occasionally, performing dedicated inspection sessions is omitted when performing inspections.

Planning

Among other things, the goal of the inspection, the work results that are to be inspected, and the roles and participants are determined during the planning phase.

Overview

In the overview phase, the author explains the requirements to be inspected to all team members so that there is a common understanding about the requirement among all inspectors.

Error detection

In the error detection phase, the inspectors search through the requirement for errors. Error detection can be performed individually by each inspector or collaboratively in a team. Individual inspection has the advantage that each inspector can concentrate on the requirements. On the other hand, team inspections have the advantage that communication between the inspectors creates synergy effects during error detection. During the course of error detection, any errors that are found are purposively documented.

Error collection and consolidation

In the error collection phase, all identified errors are collected, consolidated, and documented. During consolidation, errors that have been identified multiple times or errors that aren't really errors are identified. The latter can be the case if, for instance, an inspector makes wrong assumptions about a requirement or interprets some constraint the wrong way. Along with consolidation, the identified errors and correcting measures are documented in an error list. Inspections are also known as *technical reviews*.

Roles during inspection

For an inspection to be performed, the following roles must be staffed with suitable personnel:

- *Organizer:* The organizer plans and supervises the inspection process.
- *Moderator:* The moderator leads the session and ensures that the pre-determined inspection process is followed. It is advisable to select a neutral moderator because the moderator could potentially balance out opposing opinions of authors and inspectors.
- *Author:* The author explains the requirements that he created to the inspectors in the overview phase and later on is responsible for correcting the errors identified.
- *Reader:* The reader introduces the requirements to be inspected successively and guides the inspectors through them. The role of the reader should be given to a neutral stakeholder so that the inspectors can center their attention on the requirements instead of on the interpretation of the author. Often, the moderator is also the reader.
- *Inspectors:* The inspectors are responsible for finding errors and communicating their findings to the other members of the project team.
- *Minute-taker:* This person takes minutes of the results of the inspection.

7.5.3 Walk-Through

In requirements validation, a walk-through is a lightweight version of an inspection. A walk-through is less strict than an inspection and the involved roles are differentiated to a lesser degree. During a walk-through, at least the roles of the reviewer (comparable to the inspector), author, and minute-taker, and potentially the moderator, are staffed.

Lightweight inspection

The goal of a walk-through of requirements is to identify quality flaws within requirements by means of a shared process and to gain a shared understanding of the requirements between all the people involved. To prepare for a walk-through, the requirements to be validated are handed out to all participants and inspected. During the walk-through session, the participants discuss the requirements to be validated step-by-step, under guidance of the moderator/reader. Usually, the author of a requirement is the one who introduces the requirement to all other participants. This way, the authors have the opportunity to give additional information to the group along with the actual requirement (e.g., alternative requirements, decisions, and rationale for decisions). A minute-taker documents the flaws in quality that have been identified during the session.

Discussion of the identified flaws in quality during a group session

7.5.4   Perspective-Based Reading

Check requirements from a defined perspective.

Perspective-based reading is a technique for requirements validation in which requirements are checked by adopting different perspectives [Basili et al. 1996]. Typically, perspective-based reading is applied in conjunction with other review techniques (e.g., during inspections or walk-throughs). Focusing on particular perspectives when reading a document verifiably leads to improved results during requirements validation. Possible perspectives for validation, for instance, emerge from the different addressees of a requirement [Shull et al. 2000]:

- *User/customer perspective:* The requirements are checked from the perspective of the customer or the user to determine whether they describe the desired functions and qualities of the system.
- *Software architect perspective:* The requirements are checked from the perspective of the software architect to ascertain if they contain all necessary information for architectural design (e.g., if all relevant performance properties have been described).
- *Tester perspective:* The requirements are checked from the perspective of the tester to establish whether they contain the information necessary to derive test cases from the requirements.

Perspective quality aspects

The three quality aspects (see section 7.3) also describe three possible perspectives for requirements validation:

- *Content perspective:* With the content perspective, the auditor verifies the content of requirements and focuses on the quality of the content of the documented requirement.
- *Documentation perspective:* With the documentation perspective, the auditor ensures that all documentation guidelines for requirements and requirements documents have been met.
- *Agreement perspective:* With the agreement perspective, the auditor checks if all stakeholders agree on a requirement, i.e., if the requirements are agreed upon and conflicts have been resolved.

In addition, further perspectives that emerge from the individual context of the development project can be created as need be.

Define validation directives for each perspective.

During perspective-based validation, each auditor is assigned a perspective (at the proper point in time) from which she reads and validates the requirement. For each perspective defined, detailed instructions for performing the validation should be laid down because the auditor might not be familiar with all relevant details of her assigned perspective. It is advisable to associate questions with each validation instruction that must be answered by the content of the requirements or by the auditor after she has read the requirement, respectively. In addition, validation instructions can be amended with a checklist that summarizes the most important content aspects that ought to be addressed by a requirement with regard to the appropriate perspective.

During the course of the follow-up to a perspective-based reading session, the results of the chosen perspective are analyzed and consolidated. On the one hand, the results of the perspective-based reading contain answers to the predefined questions, and on the other hand, open issues that the auditors noticed while reading may be present. The consolidation can be done as a group effort, similarly to a review.

Follow-up

Perspective-based reading can be both an independent technique for requirements validation and a support technique for other validation techniques, such as inspections or reviews of requirements documents by means of perspective-based reading.

Support of other techniques

7.5.5   Validation through Prototypes

Requirements validation by means of prototypes allows auditors to experience the requirements and to try them out. Experiencing requirements directly through prototypes [Jones 1998] is the most effective method to identify errors in requirements. Stakeholders can try out the prototype and compare their own idea of how the system ought to be implemented with the prototype at hand and thereby find discrepancies between their ideas and the current implementation.

Depending on the further use of the prototype, one can distinguish between throw-away prototypes and evolutionary prototypes [Sommerville 2007]. Throw-away prototypes are not maintained once they have been used. Evolutionary prototypes are developed with the goal to be developed further and improved in later steps. In contrast to throw-away prototypes, implementation plays a much more significant role here. Therefore, the effort to create evolutionary prototypes is much higher.

Evolutionary vs. throw-away prototypes

Before a prototype can be implemented, the requirements that shall be validated through the prototype must be selected. The set of requirements to be validated is limited by development resources (e.g., time, money, etc.) that can be allocated for validation. For example, a selection criterion can be the criticality of a requirement.

Selection of relevant requirements

Preparation of the validation   The following preparations have to be made in order to validate requirements by means of prototypes:

- *Manual/instructions:* The users of the prototype must be supplied with the necessary information so that they can use or apply the prototype. This can be done by means of a manual or by means of proper instruction.
- *Validation scenarios:* Validation scenarios that the users of the prototype can perform with the prototype should be prepared. A validation scenario defines, for example, all relevant data sets or user interactions.
- *Checklist with validation criteria:* For requirements validation, a checklist of validation criteria should be created according to which the prototype (and by proxy, the requirements) can be validated.

Performing the validation   The auditor should validate the prototype without being influenced; i.e., the auditor should execute the validation scenarios independently and by herself. This ensures that the validation results are created without bias.

During validation, the auditors can and ought to execute alternative and deviant scenarios and should use the prototype exploratively and experimentally once the required validation scenarios have been covered. For example, error cases that have remained hidden until then can be identified. For experimental validation of the prototype, the auditor needs to know the scope of the prototype, i.e., the set of requirements that have been considered when the prototype was created. Without knowledge of the implemented requirements, an auditor cannot decide whether an identified error can be traced back to a missing requirement or if the requirement has been consciously omitted in the prototype.

Documentation of the validation results   Requirements validation through prototypes therefore permits two types of result documentation:

- *Protocol of the auditor:* The auditor documents the results and experiences made during the validation of the prototype, e.g., by means of validation scenarios as well as a checklist that he has been supplied with.
- *Observation protocol:* The auditor can be observed by a second person. The second person creates a so-called observation protocol. This protocol can disclose additional important symptoms for errors in requirements. For example, when the auditor hesitates at a certain step in the validation scenario while using the prototype and the observer

documents this, it may be an indication for missing apparentness and as such an indication for impaired understandability of the prototype. Under certain circumstances, it may be advisable to record the validation on video because the validation situation can be analyzed in detail during the follow-up. For example, a video recording can show the realization of requirements pertaining to anthropometric properties (such as ergonomics) or intuitive use and can be investigated in detail.

The results of the validation are analyzed after validation is complete. *Analysis* Change suggestions for the requirements are consolidated. If significant changes to the requirements are necessary, it may be advisable to revise the prototype and validate anew.

7.5.6 Using Checklists for Validation

A checklist comprises a set of questions and/or statements about a certain circumstance. Checklists can be applied whenever many aspects must be considered in a complex environment and no aspect must be omitted. A checklist for requirements validation contains questions that ease the detection of errors [Boehm 1984]. Using checklists for requirements validation is very common in practice. Checklists can be used in all previously introduced techniques for requirements validation.

Before a checklist can be used, every single question or statement must *Creating checklists* be defined. The sources for questions and statements in the following list can be used to create checklists to support requirements validation:

- The three quality aspects of requirements (see section 7.3)
- Principles of requirements validation (see section 7.4)
- Quality criteria for requirements documents (see section 4.5)
- Quality criteria for individual requirements (see section 4.6)
- Experiences of the auditors from prior projects
- Error statistics [Chernak 1996]

Checklists are not necessarily complete. When using a checklist, one *Improving checklists* should always look for opportunities to improve the checklist for future use. For example, if a question was forgotten, the checklist should be amended to contain the extra question. Ambiguous questions or questions that are not understandable must be marked and revised. Outdated or no longer valid questions should be removed.

Checklists as a guideline

Checklists can support requirements validation in different ways. They can serve as a guideline for the auditor, who can follow the checklists at her own discretion (e.g., during a review).

Checklists as a means of structuring

The checklist can define a list of questions that must be strictly adhered to. These questions must be answered by the auditor to validate the requirements. In this case, the checklist serves as a measure to approach the validation in a structured manner. For example, the checklist may detail the exact process that the auditors are asked to apply, which guarantees that every auditor validates the requirements in the same way. This makes the results more comparable.

Hybrid forms of checklist application are also possible. For example, a checklist can contain obligatory questions for perspective-based reading and can contain suggestions that the auditor may or may not follow.

Successfully applying checklists

Applying checklists for requirements validation successfully depends on the manageability and complexity of the checklist. A large amount of questions can make it more difficult to use the checklist because the auditor does not have a steady overview of the questions and is thus forced to consult the checklist frequently. It is therefore advisable to design the checklist to not be longer than a single page [Gilb and Graham 1993]. In addition, questions that are formulated altogether too generically or abstractly can make it more difficult to use the checklist. For example, the question "Is the requirement formulated appropriately?" can lead to a multitude of different answers, depending on what the auditor considers an appropriately formulated requirement. The questions therefore ought to be as precise as possible.

7.6 Requirements Negotiation

To negotiate the requirements of a system to be developed, it is necessary to identify conflicts and to resolve those conflicts. This is done by means of systematic conflict management. The conflict management in requirements engineering comprises the following four tasks:

Four tasks of conflict management

- Conflict identification
- Conflict analysis
- Conflict resolution
- Documentation of the conflict resolution

These four tasks are explained in the following sections.

7.6.1   Conflict Identification

Conflicts can arise during all requirements engineering activities. For example, different stakeholders can utter contradicting requirements during elicitation.

Conflicts between requirements and conflicts between stakeholders are often not obvious due to different reasons. During the entire requirements engineering process, the requirements engineer should pay attention to potential conflicts so that they can be identified, analyzed, and resolved early on.

Conflict identification in all requirements engineering activities

7.6.2   Conflict Analysis

During conflict analysis, the reason for an identified conflict must be determined. According to [Moore 2003], different types of conflicts exist.

Determining the conflict type

A *data conflict* between two or more stakeholders is characterized by a deficit of information, by false information, or by different interpretations of some information. For example, take the following requirement: "R131: The reaction time of the planned system shall not exceed one second". A data conflict between two stakeholders with regard to this requirement can arise from the fact that one stakeholder considers a reaction time of 1 second to be too slow while another stakeholder does not believe that a reaction time of 1 second is feasibly implementable (i.e., it is too short).

Data conflict

A *conflict of interest* between two or more stakeholders is characterized by subjectively or objectively different interests or goals of stakeholders. A conflict of interest between two or more stakeholders can arise, for instance, when one stakeholder primarily focuses on keeping the costs of the planned system at a minimum while another stakeholder primarily desires a high level of quality. A conflict of interest between these two stakeholders arises when the first stakeholder rejects a requirement due to estimated costs and the second stakeholder insists on implementing it due to quality reasons.

Conflict of interest

A *conflict of value* is characterized by differing underlying values stakeholders have regarding some circumstance (e.g., cultural differences, personal ideals). For instance, a conflict of value arises when one stakeholder favors open source technologies while another stakeholder favors closed sources technologies.

Conflict of value

A *relationship conflict* is characterized by strong emotions, stereotypical relationship concepts, deficient communication, or negative inter-

Relationship conflict

personal behavior between stakeholders (e.g., insults, disrespect). For instance, a relationship conflict arises when two stakeholders of equal rank or position (e.g., department leaders) reject each other's requirements and try to distinguish themselves by forcing their requirements onto the project.

Structural conflict

A *structural conflict* is characterized by unequal levels of authority or power. For instance, a structural conflict can arise between an employee and his superior if the superior invariably rejects requirements that the employee has defined because he does not recognize the employee's competence to delineate requirements.

Mixed reasons for conflicts

Often, it is difficult to unambiguously classify emerging conflicts. For example, a conflict can be a relationship conflict with clear structural components. Similarly, a conflict of interest can be a conflict of values as well. Therefore, it is advisable to analyze an identified conflict with respect to all types so that all possible reasons for the conflict can be determined and suitable resolution strategies can be selected.

7.6.3   Conflict Resolution

Good conflict resolution is a success factor.

Conflict resolution is very important for requirements negotiation because the strategy of conflict resolution has a big influence on the willingness of the people involved (e.g., customers, consultants, or developers) to continue working together. For example, a conflict resolution considered unfair by at least one party of the conflict can lead to a decreased engagement and willingness to collaborate in the project. On the other hand, a resolution that is considered fair by all parties can increase the willingness to cooperate because this signals that everyone's ideas about the planned system are being considered.

Involvement of the relevant stakeholders

Independently from the selected resolution strategy, it is essential to involve all relevant stakeholders. If not all relevant stakeholders are considered, some opinions and viewpoints will remain unconsidered. The conflict will therefore only be resolved in part or incompletely. In the following paragraphs, different conflict resolution techniques are introduced.

Agreement

With the conflict resolution technique *agreement*, all conflict parties negotiate a solution to the conflict. The parties exchange information, arguments, and opinions and try to convince one another of each other's viewpoints in order to come to an agreeable solution.

Compromise

With the conflict resolution technique *compromise*, all conflict parties try to find a compromise between alternative solutions. In contrast to an agreement, a compromise consists of an amalgamation of different parts of the alternative solutions. Also, a compromise can mean that all alternative solutions as proposed thus far are discarded and entirely new solutions are creatively developed.

In the conflict resolution technique *voting*, all conflict parties vote on solution alternatives. The alternatives that are up for voting are presented to all relevant stakeholders. Each stakeholder casts her vote for an alternative and the alternative with the most votes is accepted as the resolution for the conflict.

Voting

In the conflict resolution technique *definition of variants*, the system is developed in a way that permits the definition of variants by deriving variants, by selecting parameters that define system variants, or by selecting variable system properties. This way, the system can satisfy the different interests of the stakeholders.

Definition of variants

In the conflict resolution technique *overruling*, a conflict is resolved by means of the hierarchical organization. This means that a conflict party with higher organizational rank or position wins the conflict by overruling objections of organizationally lower parties. If both parties have the same organizational rank, the conflict is resolved by a superior stakeholder or some third-party decider. This conflict resolution technique is only advisable if other resolution techniques have failed (e.g., no compromise could be found) or are not applicable due to limitations of resources (e.g., time).

Overruling

In the conflict resolution technique *consider-all-facts (CAF)*, all influencing factors of a conflict are being investigated so that as much information about the conflict can be collected as possible. This information is used during resolution. By prioritizing the influence factors, the relevance is determined. Based on the results of this technique, the plus-minus-interesting conflict resolution technique can be applied.

Consider-all-facts

In the conflict resolution technique *plus-minus-interesting (PMI)*, all positive and negative repercussions of a solution alternative are investigated so that positive and negative repercussions can be evaluated. Positive repercussions are placed in the category "plus" and negative repercussions are placed in the category "minus". Repercussions that are neither positive nor negative are placed in the category "interesting". Repercussions in the category "interesting" cannot be evaluated yet and must be investigated further to determine if their influence is positive or negative.

Plus-minus-interesting

In the conflict resolution technique *decision matrix*, a table is created that contains solution alternatives in the columns and all relevant decision criteria in the rows. The decision criteria can be identified by means of the

Decision matrix

technique "consider-all-facts". For each combination of criterion and solution alternative, an assessment is made, for instance by means of a point-scale ranging from irrelevant (0 points) to relevant (10 points). Table 7-1 shows a decision matrix.

	Solution alternative 1	Solution alternative 2	Solution alternative 3
Criterion 1	3	6	2
Criterion 2	5	4	10
Criterion 3	10	3	5
Sum	18	13	17

Table 7-1 *Decision matrix*

In order to find a solution, the sums of the columns are calculated; i.e., the assessments of the criteria of each solution alternative are summed up. The solution alternative with the highest score is accepted as the decision. In the example shown in table 7-1, this would be solution alternative 1.

7.6.4   Documentation of the Conflict Resolution

Risks of missing conflict documentation

Conflicts cannot be avoided during requirements engineering. A resolution to a conflict must always be traceably documented. If a conflict resolution is not properly documented, the following threats (among others) to the project may arise:

- *Handling conflicts repeatedly:* A certain conflict can arise a second time during the requirements engineering process. Without proper documentation of the conflict resolution, the conflict must be analyzed and resolved anew. This causes additional effort and can potentially lead to additional conflicts or abrogate previous resolutions.
- *Inappropriate conflict resolution:* During the requirements engineering process, the resolution of a conflict can turn out to be wrong or unsuitable. In this case, the conflict must be investigated and resolved anew. Without proper documentation, relevant information that has been considered during the initial analysis and resolution can be overlooked and the new conflict resolution can once again lead to false results.

In both cases, proper documentation of the conflict and its resolution supports the requirements engineering process and ensures that relevant information already known can be considered.

7.7 Summary

The quality of the elicited and documented requirements must be assured during requirements engineering so that it can be guaranteed that the requirements meet the desires and ideas of the stakeholders adequately. Therefore, it is necessary to validate the requirements with regard to the quality of their content, their documentation, and their agreement with respect to the different stakeholders. There are different techniques that can be selected and purposively combined for requirements validation, depending on the project peculiarities and project goals. Among the most common validation techniques for requirements are the different types of requirements reviews (e.g., commenting, inspection, walk-through) as well as perspective-based reading and validation through prototypes and checklists.

For requirements negotiation, it is necessary to identify conflicts between stakeholders, analyze them, and resolve them in a suitable manner. A systematic conflict management supports analysis and resolution of the conflicts that have been identified over the course of requirements validation or other requirements engineering activities.

8 Requirements Management

Requirements management comprises purposefully assigning attributes to requirements, defining views on requirements, prioritizing requirements, and tracing requirements as well as versioning requirements, managing requirements changes, and measuring requirements. Requirements management includes the management of individual requirements as well as the management of requirements documents.

8.1 Assigning Attributes to Requirements

Information about the requirements must be documented throughout the entire life cycle of a system. This includes, for example, unique identifiers of a requirement, the name of the requirement, the author and sources of the requirement, and the person responsible for the requirement.

8.1.1 Attributes for Natural Language Requirements and Models

To document information about requirements, it has proven useful to delineate this information in a structured manner: as attributes. Attributes of a requirement are defined by a unique name, a short description of the contents, and the set of possible values that can be assigned to the attribute.

The simplest way to define requirement attributes is by means of a table structure (template). The template defines the relevant information that is to be documented. This information, i.e., the defined attributes (attribute types), can be different for each type of requirement. For example, the template for functional requirements can be different from the template for quality requirements with respect to the defined attribute types and/or the allowed attribute values.

Template-based assignment of attributes to requirements

8.1.2   Attribute Scheme

The set of all defined attributes for a class of requirements (e.g., functional requirements, quality requirements) is called an attribute scheme. Attribute schemes are usually tailored to meet the individual project's needs.

Assignment of requirement attributes

During the course of the project, the attributes of the requirements are assigned with fitting attribute values. Figure 8-1 shows an exemplary assignment of attributes for a requirement including the attributes "identifier", "name", and "requirement description" as well as attributes that allow for documenting the stability of the requirements and its source as **well as its author.**

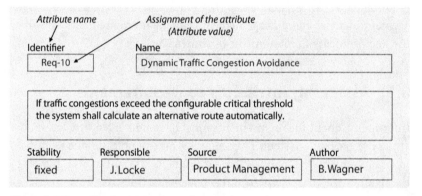

Figure 8-1 *Example of requirement attribute assignment*

The requirement that is documented on the basis of the simple template shown in figure 8-1 has the code "Req-10" as its unique identifier. It bears the name "Dynamic Traffic Congestion Avoidance" and a description that specifies the subject of this requirement. The stability of this requirement is classified as "fixed", "J. Locke" is the person responsible for this requirement, and the requirement stems from the source "Product Management". "B. Wagner" is the author.

The reader of the requirement (e.g., the contractor, product manager, developer, project manager) has a significant advantage when template-based documentation is used, namely that information of the same type can always be found in the same position (e.g., the requirement stability is always in the template section "stability"). In addition, template-based assignment of attributes has the advantage for the requirements engineer that it is harder for her to overlook important information and that this information, supported by the structure of the template and the predetermined attribute values, can be documented purposefully and correctly.

8.1.3   Attribute Types of Requirements

The various standards in requirements engineering and the most pertinent tools for requirements documentation and management often offer a set of predefined attributes. Table 8-1 lists attribute types that are frequently used in practice during requirements management.

Frequently used attribute types

Attribute Type	Meaning
Identifier	Short, unique identifier of a requirement artifact from the set of all regarded requirements.
Name	Unique, characterizing name.
Description	Briefly describes the content of the requirement.
Version	Current version of the requirement.
Author	Specifies the author of the requirement.
Source	Specifies the source or sources of the requirement.
Stability	Specifies the approximate stability of the requirement. The stability is the amount of changes that are to be expected with regard to the requirement. Possible values can be "fixed", "established", and "volatile".
Risk	Specifies the risk based on an estimate of the amount of damage and loss and the probability of occurrence.
Priority	Specifies the priority of the requirement regarding the chosen prioritization properties, e.g., "importance for market acceptance", "order of implementation", "loss/opportunity cost if not implemented".

Table 8-1 *Frequently used attribute types*

Along with the requirements attributes listed in table 8-1, many additional attribute types exist to document important information of a requirement. Table 8-2 shows a selection of additional attribute types for requirements.

Additional attribute types for requirements

Attribute Type	Meaning
Person responsible	Specifies the person, group of stakeholders, organization, or organizational unit that is responsible for the content of the requirement.
Requirement type	Specifies the type of requirement (e.g., "functional requirement", "quality requirement", or "constraint") depending on the applied classification scheme.
Status regarding the content	Specifies the current status of the content of the requirement, e.g., "idea", "concept", "detailed content".
Status regarding the validation	Specifies the current status of the validation, e.g., "unvalidated", "erroneous", "in correction".
Status regarding the agreement	Specifies the current status of the negotiation, e.g., "not negotiated", "negotiated", "conflicting".
Effort	Estimated/actual effort to implement the requirement
Release	The designation of the release in which the requirement shall be implemented.
Legal obligation	Specifies the degree of legal obligation of the requirement.
Cross references	Specifies relations to other requirements, for example, if it is known that the implementation of the requirement requires prior implementation of another requirement.
General information	In this attribute, arbitrary information that is considered relevant can be documented, for example, if the negotiation of this requirement is scheduled for discussion during the next meeting with the stakeholders.

Table 8-2 *Additional types of requirement attributes*

Project-specific tailoring of the attribute scheme

The attribute types suggested are the basis for defining an attribute scheme in the development project. To define an attribute scheme, at least the following specific aspects must be considered:

- Specific properties of the project, e.g., project size, local or distributed development, or project risk
- Constraints of the organization, e.g., organizational standards and regulations
- Properties and regulations of the application domain, e.g., reference models, modeling guidelines, standards
- Constraints and restrictions of the development process, e.g., liability law, process standards

When employing tools for requirements management, defining the attribute structure of requirements is often not done by means of tables, but is model based, by means of information models. A model-based definition of an attribute scheme determines the attribute types as well as limitations in attribute values, similar to template-based definitions. In addition, model-based attribute scheme definition allows for determining relations between attribute types of different attribute schemes.

Definition of attributes by means of information models

   Along with the advantages of table-based definition, model-based assignment of requirement attributes additionally allows consideration of requirement dependencies when selectively accessing the requirements. This aids in maintaining consistency in the attributes of the requirements. Furthermore, the information model of a model-based assignment of requirement attributes can serve as the foundation for the definition of an attribute structure to be used in a requirements management tool. (see section 9.3). Also, templates for the assignment of requirement attributes can be generated on the basis of the information model.

Advantages of model-based attributing

8.2   Views on Requirements

Structuring requirements by means of information models allows for generating specific views on requirements. It can be seen in practice that the amount of requirements and the amount of dependencies among requirements are evermore increasing. In order to keep the complexity of the requirements manageable for the project staff, it is necessary to selectively access and thereby filter the requirements depending on the current task.

   Views on requirements are often defined for different roles in the development process. Examples include views for the architect, the programmer, the project manager, and the tester. It is common to define multiple views for a role in order to support the sub-activities of each role. One particular view can also be applied to multiple roles.

Role-specific definition of views

8.2.1   Selective Views on the Requirements

A view contains a part of all available requirement information. A view can do the following:

- Select particular requirements; i.e., not every requirement is contained in a view.

▨ Mask certain attributes of requirements; i.e., not every attribute of a requirement is contained in a view.

▨ Arbitrarily combine both these selection principles; i.e., only a subset of all available requirements and only a subset of all available attributes are contained in a view.

Generating selective views Figure 8-2 illustrates the generation of three views, represented by a table that is defined on the basis of the structure of the attributes. In all three cases, the views are created by selecting attribute types as well as by determining the attributes that must be available. The definition of the first view (❶), for example, determines that only those requirements are selected that "J. Locke" is responsible for and that have a stability of "fixed". Of all selected requirements, only the attributes "identifier", "name", "description", and "author" are being considered.

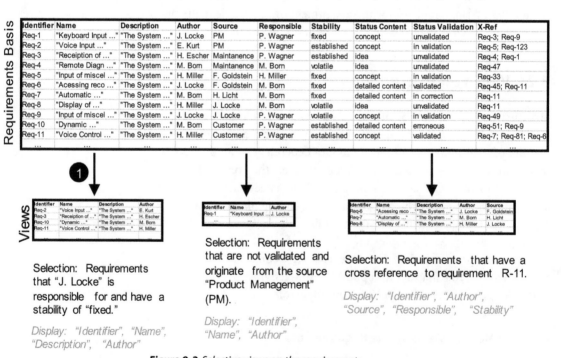

Requirements Basis

Identifier	Name	Description	Author	Source	Responsible	Stability	Status Content	Status Validation	X-Ref
Req-1	"Keyboard Input ..."	"The System ..."	J. Locke	PM	P. Wagner	fixed	concept	unvalidated	Req-3; Req-9
Req-2	"Voice Input ..."	"The System ..."	E. Kurt	PM	P. Wagner	established	concept	in validation	Req-5; Req-123
Req-3	"Reception of ..."	"The System ..."	H. Escher	Maintanence	P. Wagner	established	idea	unvalidated	Req-4; Req-1
Req-4	"Remote Diagn ..."	"The System ..."	M. Born	Maintanence	M. Born	volatile	idea	unvalidated	Req-47
Req-5	"Input of miscel ..."	"The System ..."	H. Miller	F. Goldstein	H. Miller	fixed	concept	in validation	Req-33
Req-6	"Acessing reco ..."	"The System ..."	J. Locke	F. Goldstein	M. Born	fixed	detailed content	validated	Req-45; Req-11
Req-7	"Automatic ..."	"The System ..."	M. Born	H. Licht	M. Born	fixed	detailed content	in correction	Req-11
Req-8	"Display of ..."	"The System ..."	H. Miller	J. Locke	M. Born	volatile	idea	unvalidated	Req-11
Req-9	"Input of miscel ..."	"The System ..."	J. Locke	J. Locke	P. Wagner	volatile	concept	in validation	Req-49
Req-10	"Dynamic ..."	"The System ..."	M. Born	Customer	P. Wagner	established	detailed content	erroneous	Req-51; Req-9
Req-11	"Voice Control ..."	"The System ..."	H. Miller	Customer	P. Wagner	established	concept	validated	Req-7; Req-81; Req-6
...	...	...	...	...	...	...	...	...	...

Views

❶

Identifier	Name	Description	Author
Req-2	"Voice Input ..."	"The System ..."	E. Kurt
Req-3	"Reception of ..."	"The System ..."	H. Escher
Req-10	"Dynamic ..."	"The System ..."	M. Born
Req-11	"Voice Control ..."	"The System ..."	H. Miller

Selection: Requirements that "J. Locke" is responsible for and have a stability of "fixed."

Display: "Identifier", "Name", "Description", "Author"

Identifier	Name	Author
Req-1	"Keyboard Input ...	J. Locke
...		

Selection: Requirements that are not validated and originate from the source "Product Management" (PM).

Display: "Identifier", "Name", "Author"

Identifier	Name	Description	Author	Source
Req-6	"Acessing reco ...	"The System ..."	J. Locke	F. Goldstein
Req-7	"Automatic ..."	"The System ..."	M. Born	H. Licht
Req-8	"Display of ..."	"The System ..."	H. Miller	J. Locke

Selection: Requirements that have a cross reference to requirement R-11.

Display: "Identifier", "Author", "Source", "Responsible", "Stability"

Figure 8-2 *Selective views on the requirements*

8.2.2   Condensed Views on the Requirements

Along with selecting existing information from the requirements basis, views can contain generated or condensed data that is not immediately contained in the requirements. Views that contain only generated or condensed data are called condensed views.

Condensed views can be defined by aggregating the data contained in the requirements basis. A condensed view can, for example, contain information on the percentage of requirements that stem from a particular source.

Generating condensed views

A single view may also consist of a combination of generated, condensed, and selected data.

Combination of selecting and condensing

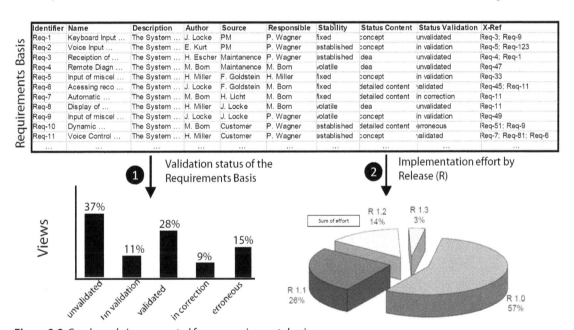

Identifier	Name	Description	Author	Source	Responsible	Stability	Status Content	Status Validation	X-Ref
Req-1	Keyboard Input ...	The System ...	J. Locke	PM	P. Wagner	fixed	concept	unvalidated	Req-3; Req-9
Req-2	Voice Input ...	The System ...	E. Kurt	PM	P. Wagner	established	concept	in validation	Req-5; Req-123
Req-3	Receiption of ...	The System ...	H. Escher	Maintanence	P. Wagner	established	idea	unvalidated	Req-4; Req-1
Req-4	Remote Diagn ...	The System ...	M. Born	Maintanence	M. Born	volatile	idea	unvalidated	Req-47
Req-5	Input of miscel ...	The System ...	H. Miller	F. Goldstein	H. Miller	fixed	concept	in validation	Req-33
Req-6	Acessing reco ...	The System ...	J. Locke	F. Goldstein	M. Born	fixed	detailed content	validated	Req-45; Req-11
Req-7	Automatic ...	The System ...	M. Born	H. Licht	M. Born	fixed	detailed content	in correction	Req-11
Req-8	Display of ...	The System ...	H. Miller	J. Locke	M. Born	volatile	idea	unvalidated	Req-11
Req-9	Input of miscel ...	The System ...	J. Locke	J. Locke	P. Wagner	volatile	concept	in validation	Req-49
Req-10	Dynamic ...	The System ...	M. Born	Customer	P. Wagner	established	detailed content	erroneous	Req-51; Req-9
Req-11	Voice Control ...	The System ...	H. Miller	Customer	P. Wagner	established	concept	validated	Req-7; Req-81; Req-6
...	...	...	...	...	...	...	...	...	...

Figure 8-3 *Condensed view generated from a requirements basis*

Figure 8-3 shows two condensed views of the requirements. The view "Validation status of the Requirements Basis" (❶) groups requirements according to the current status of validation and calculates the percentage value of the requirements with regard to the status "unvalidated", "in validation", "validated", "in correction", and "erroneous". The result is depicted as a bar chart in the figure above. In view (❷), "Implementation effort by Release", the estimated and actual effort involved with the implementation of the requirements of a particular release is depicted. In order to calculate this aggregated data, the requirements are grouped by their respective release and their implementation effort is summed up. The result is depicted as a pie chart in figure 8-3.

8.3   Prioritizing Requirements

Requirements are prioritized during requirements engineering using different prioritization criteria in all sub-activities. Requirements can be prioritized by their order of implementation, for example. Due to the different prioritizations in the various sub-activities, the priority of a requirement can be determined by one or more attributes (e.g., priority of the contractor, priority due to urgency of implementation).

8.3.1   Method for Requirements Prioritization

Determining goal and constraints of prioritization

In order to prioritize a set of requirements, a goal (i.e., purpose) of prioritization must be defined first. In addition, the constraints of prioritization are documented, such as the availability of different stakeholders and groups thereof or the resources available for prioritization.

Determining prioritization criteria

Depending on the goal of prioritization, the criterion for prioritizing the requirements (or the combination of two or more criteria) is chosen. The following are typical examples of prioritization criteria:

- Cost of implementation
- Risk
- Damage due to unsuccessful implementation
- Volatility
- Importance
- Duration of implementation (i.e., how long it takes to be implemented)

Determining Stakeholders

Depending on the goal of prioritization and the selected prioritization criteria, it is usually necessary to involve different stakeholders in the prioritization process. By choosing appropriate stakeholders, it can be guaranteed that the required expert knowledge is available during the prioritization process. The stakeholders that ought to be involved are, depending on the goal and prioritization criteria, developers, project managers, customers, or users, for example.

In addition, the requirements to be prioritized must be selected. When *Selection of artifacts*
selecting requirements, one must make sure that the selected requirements
stem from the same level of abstraction. Prioritizing requirements from
considerably differing levels of detail will lead to inconsistent and erroneous results because stakeholders tend to assign a higher priority to
requirements at higher levels of abstraction than to more refined and concrete requirements.

On the basis of the determined properties of the prioritization (e.g., *Selection of prioritization*
constraints, criteria of prioritization, etc.), a suitable prioritization tech- *techniques*
nique or a combination of multiple techniques is selected.

8.3.2   Techniques for Requirements Prioritization

For prioritization, multiple techniques exist. The techniques mainly differ
with regard to the time and effort needed but also with regard to the suitability of the different prioritization criteria and project properties.

The spectrum of prioritization techniques spans from simple, single- *Ad hoc techniques and*
criterion classification to elaborate analytic prioritization approaches, *analytical techniques*
such as AHP (Analytical Hierarchy Process) [Saaty 1980], Cost-Value-
Analysis [Karlsson and Ryan 1997], or QFD (Quality Function Deployment) [Akao 1990].

In many projects, simple ad hoc prioritization techniques such as
ranking or requirements classification are well suited. Especially with
regard to the resources available, using ad hoc techniques is often advisable.

If the decision process is considered too incomprehensible, or if the
results are too erroneous, analytical approaches for prioritization should
be used (additionally). In practice, multiple prioritization techniques are
used in combination in order to prioritize the requirements [Lehtola and
Kauppinen 2006].

Ranking and Top-Ten Technique

Two well-established techniques for requirement prioritization are, for
example, the following [Lauesen 2002]:

▨ *Ranking:* In this technique, a number of selected stakeholders arrange
   the requirements to be prioritized with respect to a specific criterion.
▨ *Top-Ten Technique:* In this technique, the n most important requirements for a defined criterion are selected. For these requirements, a

ranking order is determined afterward. This ranking order represents the importance of the selected requirements with regard to the defined criterion.

Single-Criterion Classification

Another prioritization technique that is often used in practice is based on the classification of requirements with respect to the importance of the realization of the requirements for the system's success. This type of prioritization is based on assigning each requirement to one of the following priority classes [IEEE 830-1998]:

- *Mandatory:* A mandatory requirement is a requirement that must be implemented at all costs or else the success of the system is threatened.
- *Optional:* An optional requirement is a requirement that does not necessarily need to be implemented. Neglecting a few requirements of this class does not threaten the success of the system.
- *Nice-to-have:* Nice-to-have requirements are requirements that do not influence the system's success if they are not implemented.

In practice, differentiating between "optional" and "nice-to-have" requirements can be very difficult. Therefore, requirements classification demands classification criteria that are as objectively verifiable as possible.

Kano Classification

The Kano approach introduced in section 3.2 also supports the prioritization of requirements. By making use of the Kano approach, one can classify and prioritize requirements with respect to their acceptance on the market. In order to do so, the following three property classes (see also figure 3-1) are classified:

The three properties in the Kano approach

- *Dissatisfiers:* A requirement specifies a dissatisfier the system must possess in order to be successfully introduced to the market.
- *Satisfiers:* A requirement specifies a satisfier if the customers consciously demand the associated property. Satisfiers of the system specify the degree of satisfaction of the customer. An increase in the number of satisfiers usually leads to increased customer satisfaction.
- *Delighters:* A requirement specifies a delighter if the customers do not consciously demand the defined system property or the customers do not expect the implementation of the property. The customer satisfaction increases exponentially by implementing delighters.

On the basis of requirements classified according to Kano, a prioritization of the requirements can be performed in order to plan the system releases, for example.

Prioritization Matrix According to Wiegers

The prioritization matrix according to Wiegers [Wiegers 1999] is an analytical prioritization approach for requirements. The core of the approach is a prioritization matrix according to which the priorities of the regarded requirements can be determined systematically. Figure 8-4 shows the structure of a prioritization matrix according to Wiegers as well as the method according to which priorities are calculated.

Computing requirement priorities

Relative weight ①	→2 (WeightBenefit)	→1 (WeightDet-riment)			→1 (WeightCost)		→0.5 (WeightRisk)			
Require-ment ②	Relative Benefit	Relative Detriment	Total	Value %	Relative Cost	Cost %	Relative Risk	Risk %	Priority	Rank
R_1	5	3	13	16.8	2	13,3	1	9,1	0.941	1
R_2	9	7	25	32.5	5	33,3	3	27,2	0.692	3
R_3	5	7	17	22.1	3	20,0	2	18,2	0.759	2
R_4	2	1	5	6.5	1	6,7	1	9,1	0.577	4
R_5	4	9	17	22.1	4	26,7	4	36,4	0.489	5
Total	25	27	77	100	15	100	11	100	—	
	③	④	⑤		⑥		⑦		⑧	⑨

Figure 8-4 *Calculation of priorities in a prioritization matrix according to Wiegers*

In the following, the calculation of priorities in a prioritization matrix according to Wiegers is only briefly sketched. More detailed information can be found in [Wiegers 1999].

Systematic method to determine the requirement priorities

The calculation of priorities in a prioritization matrix according to Wiegers can be done as follows:

❶ Determine the relative weights for benefit, detriment, cost, and risk.
❷ Determine the requirements to be prioritized.
❸ Estimate the relative benefit.
❹ Estimate the relative detriment.
❺ Calculate the total values and percentage values for each requirement:

$Value\%(R_i) =$
$Benefit(R_i) \times WeightBenefit + Detriment(R_i) \times WeightDetriment$

❻ Estimate the relative cost and calculate the cost percentage for each requirement.

❼ Estimate the relative risks and calculate the risk percentage for each requirement.

❽ Calculate the individual requirement priorities:

Priority(R$_i$)=
Value%(R$_i$)/(Cost%(R$_i$) × WeightCost + Risk%(R$_i$) × WeightRisk)

❾ Assert the rank of the individual requirements.

It became apparent in practice that analytical prioritization approaches such as the prioritization matrix according to Wiegers as sketched above demand considerably more time and effort than ad hoc approaches, so these ad hoc approaches are to be favored in many cases. However, analytical approaches have the advantage that the degree of subjectivity in the prioritization results can be significantly reduced so that they lead to more objective and comprehensible results in complex and critical prioritization situations.

8.4   Traceability of Requirements

An important aspect of requirements management is ensuring the traceability of requirements. The traceability of a requirement is the ability to trace the requirements over the course of the entire life cycle of the system (see section 4.5.5).

8.4.1   Advantages of Traceable Requirements

Advantages of requirements traceability

The use of traceability information supports system development in many aspects and is often the precondition for establishing and using certain techniques during the developmental process [Pohl 1996; Ramesh 1998]:

▪ *Verifiability:* Traceability of requirements allows verifying whether a requirement has been implemented in the system, i.e., if the requirement has been implemented through a system property.

▪ *Identification of gold-plated solutions in the system:* Traceability of requirements allows for the identification of so-called gold-plated solutions of the developed system and thereby allows identifying unneeded properties. In order to do that, for each system property (functional or qualitative), a check is performed to determine whether it contributes to the implementation of a requirement of the system.

- *Identification of gold-plated solutions in the requirements:* Tracing requirements back to their origin allows identifying requirements that do not contribute to any system goal and are not associated with any source. Usually, there is no reason for these requirements to exist and hence these requirements do not have to be implemented.
- *Impact analysis:* Traceability of requirements allows for the analysis of effects during change management. For example, traceability of requirements allows identifying the requirements artifacts that must be changed when their underlying requirements undergo a change.
- *Reuse:* Traceability of requirements allows for the reuse of requirements artifacts in other projects. By comparing the requirements of a previous project to the requirements of a new project by means of trace links, development artifacts (e.g., components, test cases) can be identified that may be adapted and/or reused in the new development project.
- *Accountability:* Traceability of requirements allows for retroactive assignment of development efforts to a requirement. After the requirement is implemented, for example, all partial efforts for the associated development artifact can be summed up and associated with the requirement.
- *Maintenance:* Traceability of requirements allows for simplified system maintenance. For example, the cause and effect of failures can be identified, the system components that are affected by the failure can be determined, and the effort for removing the underlying error can be estimated.

8.4.2 Purpose-Driven Definition of Traceability

As resources are usually severely restricted during development projects, capturing all conceivable information that supports the traceability of requirements over the course of the system life cycle is almost never possible.

In order to establish requirements traceability effectively and efficiently, the information to be recorded should be chosen with respect to the purpose that it will serve. In other words, only the information which has a clear purpose for system development or system evolution [Dömges and Pohl 1998; Ramesh and Jarke 2001] ought to be recorded. Recording

Purpose of traceability information

of traceability information that is not purpose driven often results in the fact that the recorded information cannot be profitably used in the development project. Traceability information that is recorded in this fashion is often sketchy and incomplete, unstructured, and erroneous with regard to its further use.

8.4.3   Classification of Traceability Relations

Pre-RS traceability and post-RS traceability

The pertinent literature on the topic of requirements traceability suggests different kinds of traceability of requirements. A common differentiation is distinguishing between pre-requirements-specification (pre-RS) traceability and post-requirements-specification (post-RS) traceability of requirements [Gotel and Finkelstein 1994]. We thus distinguish between three kinds of traceability:

- *Pre-RS traceability:* Pre-RS traceability are traceability links between requirements and those artifacts that are the basis for the requirements, e.g., artifacts like the source or origin of a requirement (previous artifacts).
- *Post-RS traceability:* Post-RS traceability comprises traceability information between requirements and artifacts of subsequent development activities. For example, such artifacts could be components, implementation, or test cases that belong to a requirement (posterior artifacts).
- *Traceability between requirements:* The traceability between requirements is about mapping dependencies between requirements. An example of this kind of traceability is the information that a requirement refines another requirement, generalizes it, or replaces it.

Figure 8-5 shows the three types of traceability of requirements in requirements engineering.

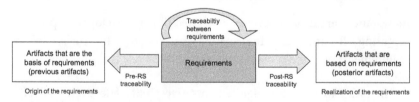

Figure 8-5 *Types of requirements traceability*

Figure 8-6 shows the three types of requirements traceability by means of requirement "R-14" in an example. The pre-RS traceability comprises the relations of requirement "R-14" to its origin. The origin of this requirement are the artifacts in the system context that influence the requirement. The post-RS traceability of requirement "R-14" consists of the relations to the components in the rough design, the refined design, and the respective implementation as well as test cases that are used during system testing and verify the implementation of the requirement in the developed system.

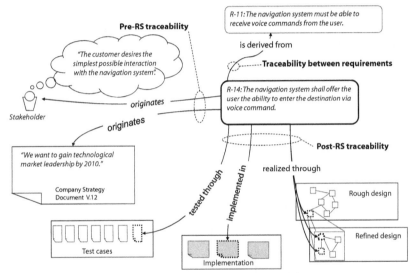

Figure 8-6 *Example of the three types of requirements traceability*

In addition, figure 8-6 shows the traceability between requirements. The traceability link between requirement "R-14" and "R-11" documents that requirement "R-14" was derived from requirement "R-11".

8.4.4   Representation of Requirements Traceability

Requirements traceability information can be represented in different ways. The most common approaches to representing traceability are simple textual references, hyperlinks, and trace matrices and trace graphs.

Text-Based References and Hyperlinks

This simple way to represent traceability information of a requirement consists of annotating the target artifact as a textual reference in the requirement (initial artifact) or to establish a hyperlink between the initial artifact and the target artifact. When linking artifacts, different types of hyperlinks with specific link semantics can be used.

Trace Matrices

Another common technique for representing and documenting traceability information between requirements as well as between requirements and previous and posterior artifacts in the development process are trace matrices. The rows in a trace matrix contain the initial artifacts (requirements). In the columns, the target artifacts (e.g., sources of requirements, development artifacts, requirements) are represented. If a trace link exists between an initial artifact in row *n* and a target artifact in column *m*, cell *(n, m)* is marked in the trace matrix.

Interpretation of a trace matrix

Figure 8-7 shows a simple trace matrix for the trace relation "derived" that exists between two requirements. An entry in the matrix specifies that a trace link of type "derived" exists from a requirement "*Req-n*" to another requirement "*Req-m*" such that "*Req-n*" was derived from "*Req-m*".

Target artifacts

derived	Req-1	Req-2	Req-3	Req-4	Req-5
Req-1		X			
Req-2			X		
Req-3					X
Req-4			X		
Req-5					

Initial artifacts

Figure 8-7 *Representation of traceability information in a trace matrix*

Maintainability of trace matrices

In practice, it became apparent that trace matrices are difficult to maintain as the number of requirements increases. A trace matrix that, for example, documents the refinement relations between merely 2,000 requirements contains over four million cells. In addition, many trace matrices must be created in order to be able to represent the available information cleanly (e.g., with regard to different types of traceability links).

Trace Graphs

A trace graph is a graph in which all nodes represent artifacts and all edges represent relationships between artifacts. The distinction between different artifacts and types of traceability can be realized by means of assigning different attributes to the nodes and edges of the graph.

Figure 8-8 shows the representation of traceability information in a simple example. In the trace graph, a node type is defined for each type of artifact (context information *"C"*, requirements *"Req-n"*, components *"Comp-n"*). In addition, three types of edges are defined to represent three types of traceability relations *("realized through", "is origin", "refines")*.

Trace graph over different development artifacts.

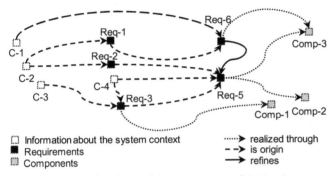

Figure 8-8 *Representation of traceability in a trace graph (extract)*

If traceability information about previous artifacts (e.g., stakeholders and interview protocols) as well as posterior artifacts (e.g., test cases and components) must be managed, traceability chains for the respective requirement can be created at different levels, up to a trace of the requirement over the entire life cycle of the system. Common tools to maintain requirements allow for the definition of representation levels when creating traceability chains so that, depending on the selected level, only immediate relations of a requirement or entire traceability chains for the requirement can be generated and displayed. The traceability chains are the foundation for a comprehensive impact analysis during requirements change management.

Traceability chains

8.5   Versioning of Requirements

During the life cycle of a system, the requirements of the system change as new requirements are added and existing requirements are removed or altered. The reasons for changes in requirements are diverse. One possible reason is, for instance, the fact that stakeholders learn more and more about the system as requirements engineering progresses. As a result, new

Subject of version control

and altered requirements come to their mind. Due to these changes, a suitable versioning of requirements is strongly advisable.

Versioning of requirements aims at providing access to the specific change states of individual requirements over the course of the life cycle of the system. The version of a requirement is defined by its specific content of the change state and is marked by a unique version number. The information that is subject to version management can be single text-based requirements, sentences, sections of requirements documents, or entire requirements documents, but also requirements models and partial requirements models.

8.5.1 Requirements Versions

When versioning requirements, one can distinguish between the version and the increment of the version number. For example, the version number 1.2 references a requirement with version 1 and the increment 2.

Figure 8-9 illustrates the method of assigning version numbers. As shown in the figure, with smaller changes regarding the content, the increment is increased by one. If larger changes are performed, the version number is incremented. If the version number is increased, the increment is set to the initial value (0). A *v* can be added in front of the version number to make it more understandable and easier to identify as such.

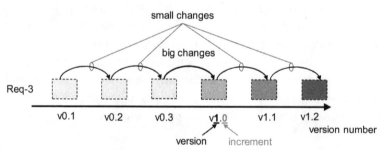

Figure 8-9 *Requirements versions*

Along with the rather simple structuring by means of version numbers, and the proposed method of versioning requirements, other methods of assigning version numbers are widely used. For example, it is possible to distinguish between the version identifier, the increment identifier, and the sub-increment identifier (v1.2.12).

8.5.2 Requirements Configurations

A requirements configuration consists of a set of requirements with the additional condition that each selected requirement is present in the requirements configuration with exactly one version, identified by the version number.

Managing configurations of requirements can be described in two dimensions [Conradi and Westfechtel 1998]: In the product dimension, configuration management deals with individual requirements within the requirements base (foundation). In the version dimension, configuration management considers the various change states as part of version management within the product dimension. Figure 8-10 illustrates both dimensions of configuration management of requirements. On the requirements axis, requirements are represented. On the version axis, the different versions of the requirements are depicted.

Dimensions of configuration management of requirements

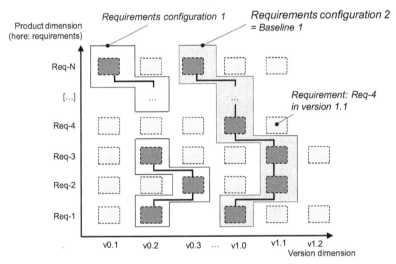

Figure 8-10 *Dimensions of configuration management of requirements (based on [Conradi and Westfechtel 1998])*

A configuration of requirements subsumes a defined set of logically connected requirements (more precisely, versions of requirements), where each requirement of the requirements base may occur at most once in the requirements configuration. A requirements configuration does not need to contain a version of every requirement that is considered in the product

Properties of requirements configurations

dimension (see figure 8-10, requirements configuration 1). A configuration of requirements has the following properties:

- *Logical connection:* The requirements contained in a configuration are directly logically connected to one another, i.e., a goal-oriented grouping of the requirements to a common configuration has been performed.
- *Consistency:* The requirements contained in a configuration do not contradict one another, i.e., the configuration contains requirements that are contradiction free in their respective version.
- *Unique identification:* A configuration has a unique identifier (ID) which can be used to uniquely identify the configuration.
- *Immutable:* A configuration defines a certain, immutable state of the specification. If requirements of a configuration are changed, a new version of the requirements and potentially of the configuration is the result.
- *Basis for rollbacks:* If changes of requirements must be undone, configurations offer the ability to roll back requirements to a specific version within a configuration. Therefore, a consistent state of the specification can be maintained.

8.5.3   Requirements Baselines

Configuration vs. baseline   Requirements baselines are specific configurations of requirements that typically comprise stable versions of requirements and, also, often define a release of a system. Due to that property, requirements baselines are usually visible externally (e.g., to the contractor). When requirements baselines are used, a number of important activities in the development process are supported:

- *Basis for release planning:* Requirements baselines are configurations of "stable" requirements, specially marked for the contractor. Baselines therefore serve as the basis of communication for the planning of system releases as well as their definition.
- *Estimation of the effort involved with implementation:* As baselines of requirements can be used for the definition of system releases, they can also be used to estimate the effort needed to realize a system release. This can be done by estimating the partial effort involved with implementing a requirement of the baseline and summing up the total effort for the remaining baseline.

■ *Comparison to competing products:* Requirements baselines can be used to compare the planned system to competing systems.

8.6   Management of Requirements Changes

Requirements change over the course of the entire development and life cycle of a system. This means that new requirements are added and existing requirements are changed or removed.

8.6.1   Requirements Changes

The reasons for changes in requirements can be multifarious. Along with changes that stem immediately from errors or incomplete requirements, the evolution of the context can make it necessary to change the requirements. For example, changes in the stakeholders' desired application of the system, amendments to a law, new technologies, or additional competition in the market can influence the requirements and make changes necessary. Changes in requirements, however, can also stem from system failure after the system was deployed if an error in the requirements can be held responsible for the failure.

Reasons for changes

Changes in requirements per se are not negative. They are merely an indication that stakeholders deal closely with the system and learn more and more about its functions, qualities, and restrictions. If change requests only occur infrequently during development of the system, it may be a sign of low stakeholder interest in the system to be developed.

Changes per se are not negative.

However, if requirements changes occur very frequently, the development of a system that is in agreement with all involved stakeholders becomes nearly impossible. A high change frequency is, among other things, an indicator for inadequately performed requirements engineering activities, such as elicitation and negotiation techniques. In addition, a high change frequency takes up a lot of resources in the development project.

Change frequency as an indicator of process quality

8.6.2   The Change Control Board

Over the course of the system life cycle, it is necessary to channel change requests for requirements and define a structured process that will lead to a justified decision about whether a change request is approved and how it is approved. Changes can pertain to individual requirements (e.g., redefining a requirement) or the entire requirements document. The evaluation of requirements changes, as well as the decision about performing the change, is usually the responsibility of a change control board. The change control board (CCB) typically has the following tasks:

Tasks of the
change control board

- Estimate the effort for performing the change (potentially commission a third party with an effort analysis).
- Evaluate change requests, e.g., with respect to the effort/benefit ratio.
- Define requirement changes or define new requirements on the basis of change requests.
- Decide about acceptance or rejection of change requests.
- Classify incoming change requests.
- Prioritize accepted change requests.
- Assign accepted change requests to change projects.

Representatives
in the change control board

In some cases, the CCB may want to delegate these tasks to another party. Decisions about changes have to be negotiated and agreed upon with the contractor and all involved stakeholders in the development project. Therefore, the change control board should consist of, among others, the following stakeholders, depending on the properties of the system to be developed and the development process:

- Change manager
- Contractor
- Architect
- Developer
- Configuration manager
- Customer representative
- Product manager
- Project manager
- Quality assurance representative
- Requirements engineer

The role of the change
manager

The chairperson of the change control board is the change manager. The change manager has the task, among other things, of mediating between parties in case of conflicts and to negotiate decisions with the respective parties. In addition, the change manager is responsible for communicating and documenting decisions.

8.6.3   The Change Request

In order to be able to manage changes of requirements during requirements engineering, they have to be documented in a purpose-oriented manner. A change request documents the desired change and contains additional information for the management of the change request.

Template for change requests

A change request should contain the following information:

- *Identifier:* The identifier makes it possible to uniquely identify a change request at any point during the life cycle of the system.
- *Title:* The title summarizes the key concern of the change request in one brief statement.
- *Description:* The description documents the requirement change as precisely as possible. It can contain information on the effect of the changes as well.
- *Justification:* The most important reasons as to why the change is necessary are listed here.
- *Date filed:* The date at which the change request was filed.
- *Applicant:* The name of the person that issued the change request.
- *Priority (in the applicant's opinion):* The importance of the change request according to the applicant's opinion.

Change information

In addition to the preceding change information, the following information for requirements change management is helpful:

Management information for the change request

- *Change validator:* The person that verifies if the change has been performed correctly.
- *Impact analysis status:* Flags whether an impact analysis has already been performed on the change request.
- *CCB decision status:* Flags whether the change control board has already decided upon the change request.
- *CCB priority:* Documents the priority of the change request assigned by the change control board.
- *Responsible:* Documents the person that is in charge of performing the change request.
- *System release:* Documents in which system release the changed requirement shall be implemented.

8.6.4   Classification of Incoming Change Requests

After it has been filed, the change request is classified by the change manager and the change control board. Typically, the change manager pre-classifies incoming change requests that will be introduced, adapted (if necessary), and finally approved (or rejected) during the next change control board meeting. A change request can be classified according to the following three categories:

- *Corrective requirement change:* A change request is classified thusly if the reason for the change request is a failure of the system during its operation that can be attributed to an error in the requirements.
- *Adaptive requirement change:* A change request is thusly classified if a requested change requires the system to be amended. A possible reason for an adaptive requirement change can be a change in the system context, e.g., a new technology is available or the system boundary was altered (see section 2.2).
- *Exceptional change (hotfix):* A change request is classified as an exceptional change if the change must absolutely immediately be done at all costs. Exceptional changes can be either corrective or adaptive.

The method for processing requirements changes depends on their classification. For example, exceptional changes must be analyzed, evaluated, decided, and potentially implemented right away. Contrastingly, adaptive requirement changes are often processed in batches at a later point in time, typically as soon as the next (or some subsequent) system release is imminent. On the other hand, corrective requirement changes are usually analyzed, evaluated, and if necessary implemented rather promptly after the change request has been filed.

8.6.5   Basic Method for Corrective and Adaptive Changes

Figure 8-11 illustrates the principal method of handling change requests. This method can be tailored depending on organizational and project-specific particularities.

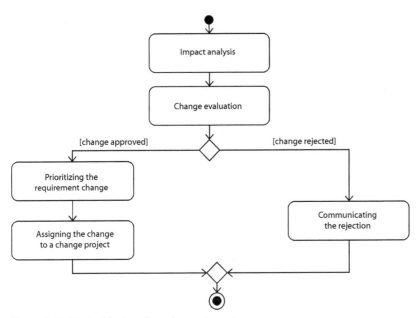

Figure 8-11 *Method for handling change requests*

During impact analysis, the effort for performing the change is estimated.   *Impact analysis*
In order to do so, all requirements affected by the change are sought out,
including any newly defined requirements. Afterward, the posterior development artifacts that potentially will have to be changed or redeveloped
are identified (e.g., test cases or components). For each affected artifact, the
effort for implementing the change is determined and the total effort for
the change is computed by summing up all partial efforts.

The consistent integration of the changes into the requirements basis
often only negligibly influence the total effort. The most significant por-
tion of the total effort is usually generated by the necessary adaptations of
the posterior development artifacts.

Identifying those requirements and posterior development artifacts   *Using traceability*
that are affected by a requirements change can be automated or at least   *information*
supported by means of traceability information. If no or not all necessary
traceability information is available, domain experts or experts of the
development team should be questioned with respect to the consequences
of the change request filed.

Evaluating a change

After the impact analysis has been completed, the change control board evaluates the change filed. In order to do that, cost and benefit are compared and evaluated with regard to the available resources. For example, the benefit of the change can be the avoided loss in prestige, improved market position, or avoided contract penalties.

Implementing approved changes

In the next step, approved changes are prioritized by the change control board. Afterward, the requirements changes are assigned to a change project or the next (or any subsequent) system release for implementation.

Validating the requirement changes

Planning, control of the implementation, and validation of the successfully applied changes are typically the responsibility of the change manager or of the change control board and may be delegated, of course.

8.7 Measurement of Requirements

Metrics can be used to assess the quality of requirements and the requirements engineering process. A metric can be used to measure one or more properties of requirements or of the requirements engineering process. The measurement results obtained by using metrics are indicators of the product and process quality.

8.7.1 Product vs. Process Metric

We thus differentiate between two types of metrics:

- Product metrics, used to obtain insights regarding the amount and quality of the documented requirements and requirements documents
- Process metrics, used to obtain insights regarding the progress and quality of the requirements engineering process

8.7.2 Examples of Product and Process Metrics

A typical example of a process metric used in requirements engineering is a metric used to measure the "requirements changes" over a period of time (e.g., already agreed-upon requirements that have been changed within one month or week).

A typical example of a product metric used in requirements engineering is a metric used to measure the "number of requirements errors" identified in a requirements specification at a given point in time. Typically, the error rate is calculated as a relative value, for example, per 100 pages of the specification or per 1000 requirements.

The rate of requirements errors is primarily an indicator of the quality of the requirements documents produced. Moreover, it is also an indicator of the quality of the requirements engineering process.

8.8　Summary

Requirements management is a core activity of requirements engineering. It's the aim of this activity to maintain persistent availability of the documented requirements as well as other relevant information over the course of the entire system or product life cycle, to structure this information in a sensible manner (e.g., by means of requirements attributes), and to ensure selective access to this information. The management of requirements comprises techniques of the following categories:

- *Assigning attributes to requirements:* In order to allow for requirements management, properties of requirements are documented by means of requirements attributes.
- *Prioritizing requirements:* Requirements are prioritized at different points in time, during different activities, and according to different criteria. Depending on the goal of prioritization and the subject of prioritization, different prioritization techniques are to be used.
- *Traceability of requirements:* During requirements management, traceability information of requirements is recorded, organized, and maintained so that information about cross references and dependencies between requirements or between requirements and other development artifacts can be used.
- *Versioning of requirements:* Versioning and configuring requirements makes it possible to keep information about specific developmental states of requirements and requirements documents available over the course of the life cycle of the system or the product.

▨ *Management of requirements changes:* Usually, the change control board is responsible for processing change requests. The change control board decides if a change request is approved or rejected and prioritizes it. The board also performs an impact analysis to estimate the impact of the change on all requirements and development artifacts as well as the resources necessary for implementing the change.

▨ *Measurement of requirements*: Product and process metrics can be used to measure the quality of the requirements and the requirements engineering process.

9 Tool Support

The different activities of requirements engineering should be supported by adequate tools that ideally integrate and continue processing the already existing information. This information could have been generated during requirements engineering (e.g., natural language or model-based requirements) or could have been used as the basis for requirements (e.g., conversation minutes, goal documents, lists of stakeholders). In practice, the most commonly known tools for requirements engineering are tools that support the management of requirements (see chapter 8). This chapter primarily considers requirements management tools (RM tools, for short). Along with RM tools, there are also tools in requirements engineering that support the elicitation, documentation, negotiation, and validation of requirements.

9.1 General Tool Support

A great number of tools that are being used during system development can also be used during requirements engineering. In that sense, test management, bug tracking, or configuration management tools often offer the ability to manage requirements or have the ability to be extended to do so. One advantage of using such tools for requirements management is that requirements can be well integrated with the artifacts the tools were originally designed to create, like test cases or change requests. For example, if requirements are managed using a test management tool and not a distinct RM tool, an interface between two tools can be omitted and tracing test cases and their respective requirements becomes much simpler.

Tools during system development

Wiki technologies are nowadays also used to support requirements engineering. For instance, glossaries can be authored collaboratively or system requirements can be worked on in cooperation using wiki technologies. Especially in case of systems with a large number of stakeholders, wikis have proven themselves as exceedingly useful in practice.

Support through wiki technologies

Tools to structure, present,
visualize, and simulate

Tools of other tool categories can help increase the effectiveness and efficiency of requirements engineering. Mind maps that have been developed during brainstorming sessions can serve as a structuring aid, and presentation tools can help in designing a rough analysis concept. If prototypes are used, simulation tools or test environments can help to simulate the operation of the system. Tools to design prototypical user interfaces (GUI prototypes) or development environments can illustrate user interfaces and functions and serve as a basis for discussion. Flow charting tools and visualization programs can be used to generate different diagrams and graphics.

Communication, office, and
project management tools

Also, tools that are commonplace in everyday work scenarios, such as office suites, can be used gainfully in requirements engineering. Mail clients, chat software, address books, calendar applications, and groupware platforms as well as tools for project management, planning, and project controlling are everyday work tools that can aid requirements engineering. These tools support stakeholders in the communication, planning, and coordination of their tasks.

9.2   Modeling Tools

Along with natural-language-based information, in requirements engineering information is also documented based on models, which can be generated using modeling tools (see chapter 6). These tools do not only offer the ability to create the models, they often also allow analyzing the models for syntactic correctness.

When choosing modeling tools, it is important to adhere to criteria similar to those for specialized requirements management tools (see section 9.5). The modeling tool must provide a unique ID to each model element to support traceability between the different models and allow for multi-user manipulation. In addition, modeling tools should offer some kind of version control functionality with regard to the models and the model elements.

Traceability between
multiple tools

An important aspect related to the application of different tools is the integration and traceability between artifacts of the different tools (e.g., use cases, behavior models, and test cases). The choice of the modeling tool or the RM tool ought to be made with regard to the interface between both tools. That means that an interface should either be already present or be easy to create. Such an interface should allow for tracing changes in models and/or requirements and for managing the traces between models and requirements (see chapter 8). If requirements change, it is indispensable to make the necessary changes in the associated model elements as well. Similarly, if a model changes, the necessary changes must be integrated into the natural language requirements as well.

9.3   Requirements Management Tools

To support requirements management techniques (as described in chapter 8) most optimally, a RM tool should have the following basic properties:

Necessary properties of RM tools

- Manage different information (e.g., natural language requirements, conceptual models, sketches, test plans, change requests)
- Manage logical relationships between information (traceability, e.g., between requirements or between requirements and their implementation)
- Allow for unique identification (e.g., a unique ID for every managed artifact)
- Edit the managed information (multi-user accessibility, access control, configuration and version management)
- Allow for different views on the managed information, depending on the purpose
- Organize the managed information (grouping, hierarchically structuring, assigning attributes, and annotation of additional information)
- Generate reports or summaries regarding the managed information (e.g., reports of change requests for requirements)
- Generate different kinds of output documents based on the managed information (e.g., generate requirements documents for a specific system release)

Depending on the amount of functions and depending on what the basic functions cover, requirements management tools can be categorized in two ways:

- Specialized tools
- Standard office applications

9.3.1   Specialized Tools for Requirements Management

Tools of this category have been developed specifically to support requirements management techniques and govern any tasks associated therewith. Characteristic properties of such tools are as follows (see chapter 8):

*Characteristic
RM tool properties*

- Management of requirements and attributes on the basis of information models
- Organization of requirements (by means of hierarchy levels)
- Configuration and version management on requirement level
- Definition of requirement baselines
- Multi-user accessibility and management (e.g., access control)
- Traceability management
- Consolidation of elicited requirements (e.g., generation of views)
- Change management support (change control)

Architecture of RM tools

The different RM tools that are available on the market possess a similar structure. The most common tools have a user interface that the user can use to access all functions necessary to carry out the requirements management tasks. The managed data is stored in a database and can be edited using an integrated editor. Different import and export functions for documents ensure that imported data from external systems can be read by the RM tool and exported data can be read by external systems.

Suitability of RM tools

Such requirements management tools thus cover most of the basic functions. They are very well suited to managing the relevant information for requirements engineering. An overview of the products that support requirements engineering and that are available on the market can be found, for example, on the website of the INCOSE and of the Volere process.

9.3.2   Standard Office Applications

In many projects, standard office applications are still used to manage requirements (e.g., word processors and spreadsheet calculators). The main reasons for this are that on one hand, such applications are very widely distributed, and on the other hand, no additional effort must be spent to become familiar with them. In conjunction with using templates – like, for instance, templates for requirements documentation (see section 5.2) – these applications are suited for documenting and, to some extent, for managing requirements (e.g., traceability relations can be established by means of hyperlinks).

However, such tools support the basic functions of requirements management only to a limited extent. They do not offer a version control mechanism on the level of requirements, nor do they have supporting features for specific techniques for requirements management (e.g., the ability to maintain traceability links between individual artifacts in an automated way). Some of the basic functions can be emulated using other tools. For instance, an office application that is used in conjunction with some version control tool may fulfill the requirement of active version control or managed multi-user access. Nevertheless, the productivity and performance with regard to requirements management that can be achieved with specialized tools cannot be achieved using standard office applications.

Office applications give only little support.

9.4   Introducing Tools

Before any effort can be spent on finding a tool that supports requirements management in the best possible manner, responsibilities regarding requirements engineering should already have been delineated in the organization or in the project. In addition to the parties responsible, the techniques and processes that are necessary to achieve the goal of requirements engineering and requirements management (see chapter 8) must be defined. After all, even the most sophisticated requirements management tool is but an aid for the requirements engineer and requirements engineering.

Assign responsibility.

Only when every process and every technique has been defined and all involved people are able to follow these constraints can an evaluation of the available tools be performed. The following considerations have to be factored in when choosing and introducing tools for requirements engineering:

The tool follows the method.

- The choice and introduction of tools takes up resources in the organization. This holds not only for personnel entrusted with the introduction of a tool, but also for the future users of a tool. These efforts have to be considered during evaluation.
- In practice, it has proven problematic to introduce a tool while a development project is already in progress. While additional effort for instruction of the employees can be estimated rather well, the risks that

Consider necessary resources.

Pilot project

are associated with introducing a new tool while a project is in progress are easily underestimated. Employee resistance or deficiencies of the tool that become apparent when the tool is deployed can influence the project negatively. Such risks can be avoided by introducing new tools in pilot projects. In this pilot project, additional resources for tool introduction, employee instruction, and process tailoring should be factored in.

Evaluation ▪ A suitable tool should be determined in the context of a tool evaluation. When manufacturers are surveyed and critical "must-have" criteria are defined, potential candidates for introduction can be selected and investigated in further detail. In order to do that, a catalogue of criteria must be created that describes which requirements a tool for requirements engineering must fulfill. The tools that remain to be evaluated can then be rated according to these requirements.

Costs ▪ Costs for a tool usually exceed licensing cost alone. Typically, costs for employee instruction as well as potential tool customization and costs for support must be taken into account as well.

Instruct employees. ▪ It is necessary for the future users of the tool to know, actively shape, and master the processes and activities that they encounter during requirements engineering. The users must be instructed with regard to processes, techniques, and the respective tool support.

9.5   Evaluating Tools

Due to the many different kinds of tools that are available, evaluating tools with regard to their adequacy to support requirements engineering is very tedious and challenging in practice.

Views on tools in requirements engineering   To evaluate the tools as objectively as possible, different views on the tools in requirements engineering should be adopted. By defining different tool views, it is possible to analyze the adequacy of a tool systematically and to prioritize the tool requirements individually. Figure 9-1 shows views that could be used to evaluate tool adequacy in requirements engineering.

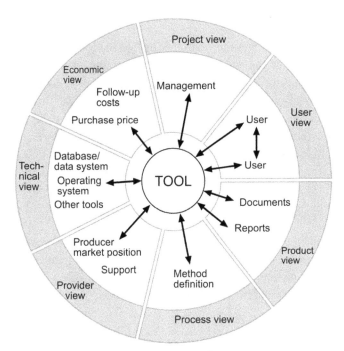

Figure 9-1 *Views on a requirements engineering tool*

For each view, criteria should be defined that are tailored toward the core aspects of the respective perspective.

9.5.1 Project View

The project view shows the extent to which the tool can support the project. Relevant criteria are support during project preparation, project planning, and project execution. With regard to project preparation, criteria can be considered that pertain to the definition of project-specific information types and documents. With regard to project planning, the scope of defined milestones as well as how information and documents that are created by means of the tool pertain to the milestones. Project execution comprises criteria that pertain to the scope of project control and project lead on the basis of information and documents that are created with the tool.

Project support

9.5.2   User View

Perspective of the future users

The user view considers the requirements for the tool that emerge out of the perspective of the users (e.g., multi-user capability). The evaluation from the perspective of the user is focused on tool usage, mapping of roles, and support of group work. In detail, this means that the different stakeholders that are involved in a development project must be adequately mapped by appropriate user management and access rights management. This enables the users to gain the appropriate access to the tool functions and the stored information, depending on their respective role.

9.5.3   Product View

Tool functions

The product view contains the functionalities that the tool possesses (e.g., different documentation types for requirements). Among other things, the supported document types, views, and reports that can be generated, as well as traceability between the selected products, are considered in this view.

9.5.4   Process View

Method support offered by the tool

The process view focuses on the method support offered by the tool (e.g., possible guidance, maintenance of traceability relations). Considerations of the process view comprise the ability to document activities within the tool as well as the extent to which the tool offers method guidance. With regard to method guidance, different degrees of obligation can be distinguished. Method guidance can be strict and restrictive or offer more lenient suggestions and hints. Along with the degree of method support that is offered by the tool, the degree to which a project-specific process model can be defined can also be considered in this view.

9.5.5   Provider View

Market position of the manufacturer and support offered

The provider view considers the market position as well as the different services that are offered by a manufacturer. When choosing a tool, not only the functional aspects but also constraints that must be fulfilled for the tool to be applicable are pertinent. The degree of brand awareness, for instance, and the reputation of the provider are therefore often used as decision criteria. Due to the relatively high acquisition cost and the long-term subscriptions to support services, a close commitment toward the provider is made.

9.5.6 Technical View

The technical view involves technical context conditions that the system is expected to meet. Important aspects in the technical view are, for instance, the ability to integrate the tool, the performance of the used repository, the necessary hardware and software, and scalability of the tool. The ability of the tool to integrate can be determined, for instance, by investigating to what extend the functionalities of the tool are accessible via an API and to what degree the process, data, and control integration is possible. The scalability of the tool can be determined, for instance, by determining the maximum number of users that can be maintained or the maximum number of objects (e.g., content packages or documents). The performance of the repository used can be measured by determining the degree to which importing and exporting data can be done as well as by determining the performance of the query interfaces or the available security concepts.

The tool's ability to perform and to integrate

9.5.7 Economic View

The economic view regards the possible costs that arise due to the acquisition, introduction, and maintenance of a tool (e.g., licensing costs, employee instruction costs, and support costs). The amount of the relevant costs can consist of the integration costs, costs of operation, maintenance and infrastructure, costs for method tailoring, and acquisition costs.

Introduction and follow-up costs

9.6 Summary

When managing requirements during requirements engineering, it is necessary to store the information in a way that the quality criteria for requirements management are met. Tools support the requirements engineer in doing so. These tools can be differentiated into professional RM tools, modeling tools, and standard office applications and differ from one another in the functionalities that are offered to the requirements engineer. This is the reason an evaluation must be done before a tool is selected, so as to not inhibit the introduction process unnecessarily.

References

[Akao 1990] Y. Akao: Quality Function Deployment – Integrating Customer Requirements into Product Design. Productivity Press, Portland, 1990.

[Bandler 1994] R. Bandler: Metasprache und Psychotherapie: Die Struktur der Magie I. Junfermann, Paderborn, 1994.

[Bandler and Grinder 1975] R. Bandler, J. Grinder: The Structure of Magic II. Science and Behaviour Books, Palo Alto CA, 1975.

[Basili et al. 1996] V. Basili, S. Green, O. Laitenberger, F. Lanubile, F. Shull, S. Sörumsgard, M. Zelkowitz: The Empirical Investigation of Perspective-Based Reading. Empirical Software Engineering, Vol. 1, No. 12, Springer-Verlag, Berlin, Heidelberg, 1996, pp. 133–144.

[Beck 1999] K. Beck: Extreme Programming Explained – Embrace Change. Addision-Wesley, Reading MA, 1999.

[Boehm 1981] B. Boehm: Software Engineering Economics. Prentice Hall, Englewood Cliffs, 1981.

[Boehm 1984] B. Boehm: Verifying and Validating Software Requirements and Design Specifications. IEEE Software, Vol. 1, No. 1, IEEE Press, Los Alamitos, 1984, pp. 75–88.

[Chaos 2006] Standish Group: Chaos Report, 2006.

[Chen 1976] P. Chen: The Entity-Relationship Specification – Toward a Unified View of Data. ACM Transactions on Database Systems, Vol. 1, No. 1, 1976, pp. 9–38.

[Chernak 1996] Y. Chernak: A Statistical Approach to the Inspection Checklist Formal Synthesis and Improvement. IEEE Transactions on Software Engineering, Vol. 22, No. 12, 1996, pp. 866-874.

[Cockburn 2001] A. Cockburn: Writing Effective Use Cases. Addison-Wesley, Reading, MA, 2001.

[Conradi and Westfechtel 1998] R. Conradi, B. Westfechtel: Version Models for Software Configuration Management. ACM Computing Surveys, Vol. 30, No. 2, 1998, pp. 232–282.

[Davis 1993] A. M. Davis: Software Requirements – Objects, Functions, and States. Prentice Hall, Englewood Cliffs, 1993.

[DeBono 2006] E. DeBono: Edward DeBono's Thinking Course: Powerful Tools to Transform Your Thinking. BBC Active, Harlow, 2006.

[DeMarco 1978] T. DeMarco: Structured Analysis and System Specification. Yourdon Press, New York, 1978.

[Dömges and Pohl 1998] R. Dömges, K. Pohl: Adapting Traceability Environments to Project-Specific Needs. Communications of the ACM, Vol. 41, No. 12, 1998, pp. 55–62.

[Easterbrook 1994] S. Easterbrook: Resolving Requirements Conflicts with Computer-Supported Negotiation. In: M. Jirotka, J. Goguen (eds.): Requirements Engineering – Social and Technical Issues, Academic Press, London, 1994, pp. 41–65.

[Elmasri and Navathe 2006] R. Elmasri, S. B. Navathe: Fundamentals of Database Systems. 5th Edition, Addison-Wesley, Reading MA, 2006.

[Gause and Weinberg 1989] D. C. Gause, M. Weinberg: Exploring Requirements – Quality before Design. Dorset House, New York, 1989.

[Gilb and Graham 1993] T. Gilb, D. Graham: Software Inspection. Addison-Wesley, Reading MA, 1993.

[Glass and Holyoak 1986] A. L. Glass, K. J. Holyoak: Cognition. Random House, New York, 1986.

[Glinz and Wieringa 2007] M. Glinz, R. Wieringa: Stakeholders in Requirements Engineering. IEEE Software 24, 2, 2007, pp. 18–20.

[Gotel and Finkelstein 1994] O. Gotel, A. Finkelstein: An Analysis of the Requirements Traceability Problem. In: Proceedings of the IEEE International Conference on Requirements Engineering (ICRE'94), 1994, pp. 94–102.

[Gottesdiener 2002] E. Gottesdiener: Requirements by Collaboration: Workshops for Defining Needs. Addison-Wesley Longman, Amsterdam, 2002.

[Harel 1987] D. Harel: Statecharts – A Visual Formalism for Complex Systems. Science of Computer Programming, Vol. 8, No. 3, 1987, pp. 231–274.

[Hatley and Pirbhai 1988] D. J. Hatley, I. A. Pirbhai: Strategies for Real Time System Specification. Dorset House, New York, 1988.

[Hickey and Davis 2003] A. M. Hickey, A. M. Davis: Elicitation Technique Selection: How Do Experts Do It? Proceedings of the 11th IEEE International Requirements Engineering Conference (RE'03), Monterey Bay, USA, 2003, pp. 169–178.

[IEEE 610.12-1990] Institute of Electrical and Electronics Engineers: IEEE Standard Glossary of Software Engineering Terminology (IEEE Std. 610.12-1990). IEEE Computer Society, New York, 1990.

[IEEE 830-1998] Institute of Electrical and Electronics Engineers: IEEE Recommended Practice for Software Requirements Specifications (IEEE Std. 830-1998). IEEE Computer Society, New York, 1998.

[ISO/IEC 9126] International Organisation for Standardization: Software Engineering – Product Quality – Part 1: Quality Model. Geneva, 2001.

[ISO/IEC 15504-5] International Organisation for Standardization: An Exemplar Process Assessment Model. Geneva, 2007.

[ISO/IEC 25010:2011] International Organization for Standardization: Systems and software engineering – Systems and software Quality Requirements and Evaluation (SQuaRE) – System and software quality models, Geneva 2011.

[ISO/IEC/IEEE 29148:2011] International Organization for Standardization: Systems and software engineering – Life cycle processes – Requirements engineering, Geneva, 2011.

[Jacobson et al. 1992] I. Jacobson, M. Christerson, P. Jonsson, G. Oevergaard: Object Oriented Software Engineering – A Use Case Driven Approach. Addison-Wesley, Reading MA, 1992.

[Jones 1998] T. C. Jones: Estimating Software Costs. McGraw-Hill, New York, 1998.

[Kano et al. 1984] N. Kano, S. Tsuji, N. Seraku, F. Takahashi: Attractive Quality and Must-be Quality. Quality – The Journal of the Japanese Society for Quality Control, Vol. 14, No. 2, 1984, pp. 39–44.

[Karlsson and Ryan 1997] J. Karlsson, K. Ryan: A Cost-Value Approach for Prioritizing Requirements. IEEE Software, Vol. 14, No. 5, IEEE Press, Los Alamitos, 1997, pp. 67–74.

[Keller et al. 1992] G. Keller, M. Nüttgens, A.-W. Scheer: Semantische Prozeßmodellierung auf der Grundlage »Ereignisgesteuerter Prozessketten (EPK)«. Publications of the institute for business informatics (IWi), Saarland University , Issue 89, Saarbrücken, 1992.

[Kosslyn 1988] S. M. Kosslyn: Imagery in Learning. In: M. Gazzaniga (ed.): Perspectives in Memory Research, The MIT Press, Cambridge, 1988.

[Kruchten 2001] P. Kruchten: The Rational Unified Process: An Introduction, Addison-Wesley, 2001.

[Laitenberger and DeBaud 2000] O. Laitenberger, J.-M. DeBaud: An Encompassing Life Cycle Centric Survey of Software Inspection. Journal of Systems and Software, Vol. 50, No. 1, 2000, pp. 5–31.

[Lauesen 2002] S. Lauesen: Software Requirements – Styles and Techniques, Addison-Wesley, London, 2002.

[Lehtola and Kauppinen 2006] L. Lehtola, M. Kauppinen: Suitability of Requirements Prioritization Methods for Market-driven Software Product Development. Software Process – Improvement and Practice, Vol. 11, No. 1, 2006, pp. 7–19.

[Macaulay 1993] L. Macaulay: Requirements Capture as a Cooperative Activity. In: Proceedings of the 1st IEEE International Symposium on Requirements Engineering, 1993, pp. 174–181.

[Maiden and Gizikis 2001] N. Maiden, A. Gizikis: Where Do Requirements Come From? IEEE Software 18, 5, 2001, pp. 10–12.

[McMenamin and Palmer 1988] S. M. McMenamin, J. F. Palmer: Essential Systems Analysis. Prentice Hall, London, 1984.

[Mealy 1955] G. H. Mealy: A Method for Synthesizing Sequential Circuits. Bell System Technical Journal, Vol. 34, No. 5, 1955, pp. 1045–1079.

[Mietzel 1998] G. Mietzel: Pädagogische Psychologie des Lernens und Lehrens. 5th Edition, Hogrefe-Verlag, Göttingen, 1998.

[Moore 1956] E. F. Moore: Gedanken-Experiments on Sequential Machines. In: C. Shannon, J. McCarthy (eds.): Automata Studies, Princeton University Press, Princeton, 1956, pp. 129–153.

[Moore 2003] C. Moore: The Mediation Process – Practical Strategies for Resolving Conflicts. 3rd Edition, Jossey-Bass, San Francisco, 2003.

[OMG 2007] OMG: Unified Modeling Language: Superstructure, Version 2.1.1. OMG document formal/2007-02-05.

[Pohl 1996] K. Pohl: Process-Centered Requirements Engineering. Research Study Press, Advanced Software Development, Taunton, Somerset, 1996.

[Pohl 2008] K. Pohl: Requirements Engineering – Grundlagen, Prinzipien, Techniken. dpunkt.verlag, Heidelberg, 2008.

[Pohl 2010] K. Pohl: Requirements Engineering – Fundamentals, Principles, and Techniques. Springer, New York, 2010.

[Pohl et al. 2005] K. Pohl, G. Böckle, F. van der Linden: Software Product Line Engineering – Foundations, Principles, and Techniques. Springer-Verlag, Berlin, Heidelberg, New York, 2005.

[Potts et al. 1994] C. Potts, K. Takahashi, A. Antón: Inquiry-Based Requirements Analysis. IEEE Software 11, 2, 1994, pp. 21–32.

[Ramesh 1998] B. Ramesh: Factors Influencing Requirements Traceability Practice. Communications of the ACM, Vol. 41, No. 12, ACM Press, 1998, pp. 37–44.

[Ramesh and Jarke 2001] B. Ramesh, M. Jarke: Toward Reference Models for Requirements Traceability. IEEE Transactions on Software Engineering 27, 1, 2001, pp. 58-92.

[Robertson 2002] J. Robertson: Eureka! Why Analysts Should Invent Requirements. IEEE Software 19, 4, 2002, pp. 20–22.

[Robertson and Robertson 2006] S. Robertson, J. Robertson: Mastering the Requirements Process. 2nd Edition, Addison-Wesley, Upper Saddle River, 2006.

[Rohrbach 1969] B. Rohrbach: Kreativ nach Regeln – Methode 635, eine neue Technik zum Lösen von Problemen. Absatzwirtschaft 12, Issue 19, 1969, pp. 73–75.

[Royce 1987] W. W. Royce: Managing the Development of Large Software Systems. In: Proceedings of the 9th International Conference on Software Engineering (ICSE'87), IEEE Computer Society Press, Los Alamitos, 1987, pp. 328–338.

[Rumbaugh et al. 2005] J. Rumbaugh, I. Jacobson, G. Booch: The Unified Modeling Language Reference Manual. 2nd Edition, Addison-Wesley, Boston, 2005.

[Rupp 2014] C. Rupp: Requirements-Engineering und -Management – Aus der Praxis von klassisch bis agil. Hanser-Verlag, Munich, 2014. (Individual chapters also available in English on the SOPHIST website: http://www.sophist.de)

[Rupp et al. 2007] C. Rupp, S. Queins, B. Zengler: UML 2 glasklar – Praxiswissen für die UML-Modellierung. Hanser-Verlag, Munich, 2007.

[Saaty 1980] T. L. Saaty: The Analytical Hierarchy Process. McGraw-Hill, New York, 1980.

[SEI 2006] *Software Engineering Institute*: CMMI for Development (CMMI-Dev), V1.2, Technical Report CMU/SEI-2006-TR-008 – ESC-TR-2006-008. Carnegie Mellon, Software Engineering Institute, Pittsburgh, PA 2006.

[Shull et al. 2000] F. Shull, I. Rus, V. Basili: How Perspective-Based Reading Can Improve Requirements Inspections. IEEE Computer, Vol. 33, No. 7, 2000, pp. 73–79.

[Sommerville 2007] I. Sommerville: Software Engineering. 8th Edition, Pearson Studium, Boston, 2007.

[Stachowiak 1973] H. Stachowiak: Allgemeine Modelltheorie. Springer-Verlag, Vienna, 1973.

[van Lamsweerde et al. 1991] A. van Lamsweerde, A. Dardenne, B. Delcourt, F. Dubisy: The KAOS Project – Knowledge Acquisition in Automated Specification of Software. In: Proceedings of AAAI Spring Symposium Series, Stanford University, American Association for Artificial Intelligence, 1991, pp. 69–82.

[V-Modell 2004] *V-Modell:* V-Modell® XT, 2004, Entwicklungsstandard für IT-Systeme des Bundes, Bundesrepublik Deutschland, Vorgehensmodell. www.kbst.bund.de

[Ward and Mellor 1985] P. Ward, S. Mellor: Structured Development of Real-Time Systems – Introduction and Tools. Vol. 1. Prentice Hall, Upper Saddle River, 1985.

[Weinberg 1978] V. Weinberg: Structured Analysis. Yourdon Press, New York, 1978.

[Wiegers 1999] K. E. Wiegers: Software Requirements. Microsoft Press, Redmond, 1999.

[Yourdon 1989] E. Yourdon: Modern Structured Analysis. Prentice Hall, Englewood Cliffs, 1989.

[Yu 1997] E. Yu: Towards Modelling and Reasoning Support for Early-Phase Requirements Engineering. In: Proceedings of the 3rd IEEE International Symposium on Requirements Engineering (RE'97), IEEE Computer Society, Los Alamitos, 1997, pp. 226–235.

Index

SOPHIST

„Grey is all theory – important is
what happens on the pitch"

Adi Preißler

**Exactly! That is why teams have to ensure the best possible
preparation for the pitch. Why not let the professional
coaches – the SOPHISTs – support you?**

We coach you in:

- eliciting and documenting system requirements.
- detecting inconsistencies and redundancies in models.
- applying notations properly and ensuring perfect modeling.
- choosing an architecture that is still valid after the
  acceptance of the product.

Presentations, trainings, consulting and coaching – we provide you
with different tatctics.
Let us keep you from running into the offside trap.

How about dicussing your personal game plan?
Just call +49 911 – 40 9000.
You can also write us an e-mail to heureka@sophist.de

www.sophist.de

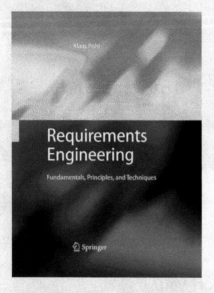

Klaus Pohl

Requirements Engineering

Fundamentals, Principles, and Techniques

Springer-Verlag 2010
Hardcover
814 pages
ISBN 978-3-642-12577-5

www.requirements-book.com

In this textbook, Klaus Pohl provides a comprehensive and well-structured introduction to the fundamentals, principles, and techniques of requirements engineering. He presents approved techniques for eliciting, negotiating and documenting as well as validating, and managing requirements for software-intensive systems. The various aspects of the process and the techniques are illustrated using numerous examples.

The book aims at professionals, students, and lecturers in systems and software engineering or business applications development. Professionals such as project managers, software architects, systems analysts, and software engineers will benefit in their daily work from the didactically well-presented combination of validated procedures and industrial experience.

Students and lecturers will appreciate the comprehensive description of sound fundamentals, principles, and techniques, complemented by a commented list of references for further reading. Lecturers will find additional teaching material on www.requirements-book.com.

The Ruhr Institute for Software Technology

www.paluno.uni-due.de/en

Printed in the USA
CPSIA information can be obtained
at www.ICGtesting.com
LVHW081331150224
771920LV00006B/555